THE
ILLUSTRATED
HISTORY
OF
Automobiles

THE
ILLUSTRATED
HISTORY
OF

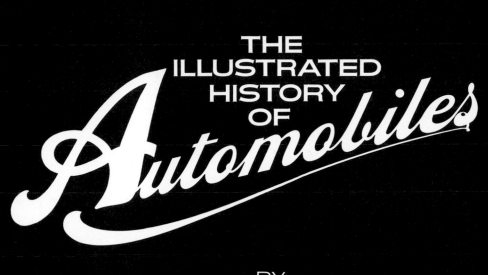

BY
DAVID BURGESS-WISE

GALAHAD BOOKS

Title page illustration: 1936 Triumph Dolomite roadster

Published in the United States of America in 1981 by A & W Publishers, Inc.
95 Madison Avenue
New York, New York 10016
By arrangement with Quarto Publishing Limited

ISBN 0 88365 483 0

This book was designed and produced by Quarto Publishing Limited, 32 Kingly Court, London W1

Phototypeset in England by Filmtype Services Limited, Scarborough
Colour separation by Sakai Lithocolour Company Limited, Hong Kong
Printed by Leefung-Asco Printers Limited, Hong Kong

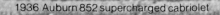

1936 Auburn 852 supercharged cabriolet

Contents

Introduction

OVER THE PAST CENTURY, the motor car industry has probably attracted more visionaries and charlatans, optimists and rogues than any other commercial activity. Today, the industry is essential to the commercial well-being of many industrialized countries—indeed, major companies can dispose of budgets far greater than those of many perfectly healthy nations.

But for every one of the few great motor companies active today, hundreds of marques

1975 Ferrari 308 GTB coupé

have run their course. For every Henry Ford and William Morris, there has been a legion of hopefuls who have formed a company, marketed perhaps a few dozen cars and then vanished into limbo, perhaps springing up with a new factory or a new marque name at another point in motoring history, their failures running a necessary counterpoint to the great success stories.

The promise of riches has attracted men of amazingly diverse backgrounds to found motor companies—hat-makers, pork-butchers,

mouth-organ salesmen and voting-machine manufacturers are some of the less likely candidates.

Out of this rich field, this book covers the most significant and entertaining marques sold—or intended to be sold—for use on the road. Cars built specifically for racing are omitted, as are specialized off-road vehicles like dune-buggies.

Illustrations have been carefully chosen to show—wherever possible—vehicles in their contemporary setting.

Having owned a Clyno—one of the great lost causes of the British motor industry—for almost 20 entertaining years, I have long realized that the companies which have failed often made better products than those which survived.

This book is, in part, a tribute to the many cheerful optimists whose products, of whatever merit, have remained up to now largely unrecorded. For my part, I have found the hunt for these obscure marques an exciting one; it has involved many hours of research, both in my own collection of automotive literature and in the unparalleled library of the Veteran Car Club of Great Britain, which, as befits the world's first old car club, has a rich collection of source material from all over the world. My visits there have garnered hundreds of obscure marques, recorded in the pages of magazines—*Automotor Journal, Horseless Age, La Vie Automobile*—as long-dead as the cars they chronicle.

This book, I hope, will bring their histories to life again.

DAVID BURGESS WISE 1979

7

Prehistory

MAN'S SEARCH FOR some form of motive power to replace the horse goes back over 300 years; clockwork, wind power and elaborate clockwork gearing were all tried before the power of steam became tractable enough to be used to drive a vehicle. Not that it was initially too successful: the oldest surviving self-propelled vehicle, Cugnot's 1770 *fardier*, owes its preservation to the fact that on its trial runs it ran amok and knocked down a wall! Put into store, it survived the French Revolution, was acquired by the Conservatoire des Arts et Métiers in Paris in 1799, and has been a major exhibit there ever since.

It was followed by a number of even less practical designs from optimistic French, English and American engineers, and it was not until 1801 that the first successful road carriage appeared. This was the work of the Cornish mining engineer Richard Trevithick and led to his London Carriage of 1803, which made a number of successful runs in the capital before it was dismantled to power a hoop rolling mill. Trevithick lacked the staying power to perfect either this or his other great invention, the railway carriage. He was succeeded by a lunatic gaggle of inventors who proposed machines driven by articulated legs, tiny railway engines running inside a drum like squirrels, compressed air, gunpowder and 'vanes, or fliers, like the sails of a windmill'.

Then, between 1820 and 1840, came a golden age of steam, with skilled engineers devising and operating steam carriages of advanced and ingenious design; men like Gurney, Hancock and Macerone all produced designs which were practicable, capable of achieving quite lengthy journeys and operating with a relatively high degree of reliability. Walter Hancock, a better mechanic than businessman, operated his steam coaches on regular scheduled services in London in the 1830s, but was rooked by his associates, and eventually called it a day after 12 years of experiment had brought him little more than unpaid debts and the hostility of those with vested interests, who, fearing that the steam carriage would prove a threat to the thousands whose livelihood depended on the horse, promoted swingeing tolls on the turnpike roads; an 1831 Parliamentary Commission, though largely favourable to the steam carriage, failed to prevent such injustices, and the final blow to the builders of steam carriages came with the advent of the railway age. Railway engines, running on smooth, level rails, had none of the problems experienced by steam carriages running on uneven, badly maintained roads, and this newer form of locomotion soon eclipsed the steam carriage, even though legislation restricting the speed and operation of steam carriages was not enacted until 1863, when it was decreed that all 'road locomotives' should have a man with a red flag walking ahead.

It was the advent of the bicycle in the 1860s which revived touring by road.

Some of the successes and failures of the prehistory of motoring: James's steam carriage (**1**) was one of the better road carriages of the early 1830s, while Dr Church's Birmingham Road Carriage (**2**) was never completed in this baroque style. The 1770 Cugnot (**3**) is the world's oldest self-propelled vehicle to survive, though it is possible that it never ran. Johann Hautsch of Nürnberg devised this curious clockwork carriage (**4**) in the seventeenth century, while the Hancock steam drag of *c*.1830 (**5**) represents the high point of early British steam carriages.

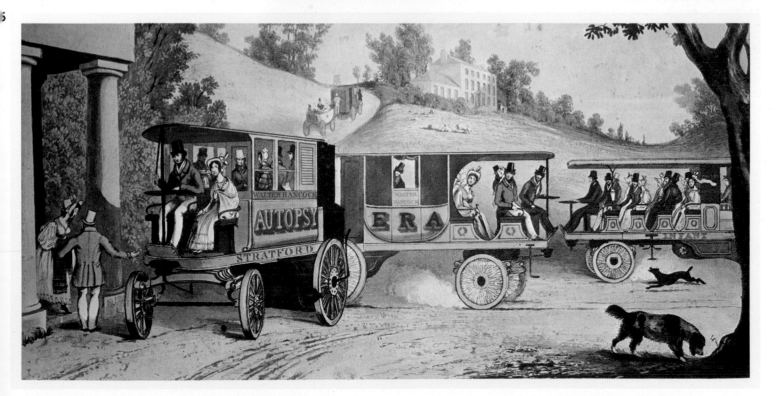

Radiators

The earliest cars, which, if they even had radiators to cool their engines, had them slung at the rear of the chassis or some other anatomically improbable position, lacked a certain amount of character. When, however, Mercedes developed the honeycomb radiator into a recognizable marque symbol, cars began to acquire personality. And, despite the hiding of the radiator behind a grille, it is still front end treatment that gives a car its character.

When Ettore Bugatti originally adopted a shape for the radiators of his cars (**1**), he apparently followed the outline of a chairback designed by his furniture-designer father, Carlo. The 1949 Bristol 400 (**2**) took its functional radiator openings from the BMW with which it was closely connected. Typical of its era, the 1913 Unic radiator (**3**) reflects honest craftsmanship, while the flamboyant frontal treatment of the 1959 Ford Fairlane Skyliner (**4**) is a product of a time when the stylist was king. On the other hand, the 1936 Railton (**5**) cloaked its American origins behind a very English radiator.

7

8

10

Like an Art Deco fencer's mask, the radiator grill of the 1936 Triumph Dolomite (**6**) is one of the more extreme designs of a decade when styling began to influence sales. But the crude front end of the 1921 Carden cyclecar (**7**) is purely a dummy, aping larger cars. The 'dollar grin' of the 1947 Buick Eight (**8**) celebrates an age of promise (of increased sales!) after World War Two; over 20 years on, a new era of restraint is marked by the bland front end of the 1970 Monteverdi 375L (**9**). The Rolls-Royce radiator (**10**) has remained true to its original design concept for over 75 years.

1880 to 1900

THE INTERNAL COMBUSTION engine appeared early in the history of the motor vehicle, but took over three-quarters of a century to be perfected to the level where it could be used in a vehicle capable of running on the roads—the 1805 powered cart of the Swiss Isaac de Rivaz was no more than an elaborate toy, only capable of crawling from one side of a room to another, and the 1863 car built in Paris by J-J. Etienne Lenoir took three hours to cover six miles. It was not until the mid-1880s that the first successful petrol cars appeared, developed independently by two German engineers, Gottlieb Daimler and Karl Benz.

Of the two vehicles, that of Benz was incontestably superior, for it was designed as an entity, using the new technology of the cycle industry, while Daimler's carriage was no more than an adapted horse vehicle. Benz went into limited production of his three-wheeled carriages (described in his catalogue as 'an agreeable vehicle, as well as a mountain-climbing apparatus') in 1888; Daimler was more interested in selling his engines as a universal power source.

Neither man found immediate success, but neither had the great geniuses of the steam vehicle who were their contemporaries. The Bollée family of Le Mans built some truly advanced steam carriages between 1873 and the mid-1880s, vehicles which pioneered independent front suspension, while blacksmith's son Léon Serpollet conceived the 'flash boiler' for instantaneous generation of steam and held the first driving licence issued in Paris. And while the Comte De Dion and his engineers Bouton and Trépardoux built some excellent steam vehicles during the 1880s and early 1890s, they were to achieve their greatest fame as manufacturers of light petrol vehicles, from 1895 on.

The crucial event in the story of the motor car was the 1889 Paris World Exhibition, for it was there that the French engineers Panhard and Levassor saw the Daimler 'Steelwheeler' car powered by the Daimler vee-twin engine. Levassor's lady friend, an astute widow named Louise Sarazin, held the French rights to the Daimler engine in succession to her late husband, and Panhard and Levassor began manufacturing these power units in 1890. They could, however, see no future for the motor car, and so granted the right to use Daimler engines in self-propelled vehicles to the ironmongery and cycle firm of Peugeot (who had just decided not to go ahead with the planned production of Serpollet steamers).

It was in France, too, that Benz enjoyed his first limited success, for his Paris agent, Emile Roger, managed to sell one or two Benz cars in Paris (and, coincidentally, garaged his first Benz in Panhard and Levassor's workshop). But it was not until his first four-wheeler, the 1893 Viktoria, that Benz began series production.

Peugeot were already established as motor manufacturers by that date, for in 1891 they had

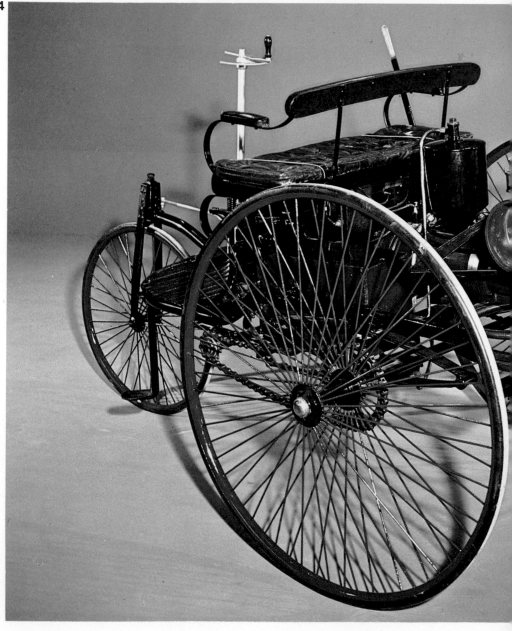

De Dion, Bouton and Trépardoux built this neat little steam car in 1885 (**1**); the lordly Bollée *Mancelle* steam carriage of 1873 (**2**) was a precursor of petrol car design, with the engine under a frontal bonnet driving the rear wheels, and independent front suspension. Indeed, the 1899 Fiat 3½hp (**3**) and its contemporaries were far more primitive in concept. The first petrol car conceived as an entity was the 1885–86 Benz three-wheeler (**4**). Serpollet's 1888 three-wheeler (**5**) used his high-speed flash boiler. The 1895 tricar (**6**) utilized the power unit from a Leyland steam lawnmower.

actually sold 5 cars, boosting production to a dizzy 29 the following year.

The success of the Peugeot cars inspired Panhard and Levassor to reconsider their early opinion of the horseless carriage, and, after building a couple of crude dogcarts with the engine at the rear, Levassor devised the famous *Système Panhard*, with the engine at the front driving the rear wheels via a sliding pinion gearbox inspired by the mechanism of a lathe, a layout which, however '*brusque et brutale*' its inventor thought it, has been used on the majority of motor cars built since.

In America, the motor car was evolving along different lines from Europe and, in January-February 1891, the New World's first petrol vehicle, a friction-driven three-wheeler built by John W. Lambert of Ohio City, made its first tentative runs. In 1895, America's first motor manufacturing company was founded by the Duryea brothers, Charles and Frank (whose prototype dated from 1893); the following year they exported a couple of vehicles to Britain. However, anti-motoring prejudice in that country was running high, and there was little encouragement for motor vehicles, either home-grown or imported (though the company promotions of the so-called 'father of the British motor industry', H. J. Lawson, succeeded in parting a good many credulous investors from a large amount of cash).

Lawson had influential friends and in 1896 succeeded in getting the ridiculous requirement for motor cars to be preceded by a man on foot (a legacy of the old Locomotives on Highways Acts of 1865 and 1878) to be repealed, and held a commemorative run to Brighton on November 14, 1896 to celebrate the raising of the speed limit to 12 mph. Some of the participating machines, though, covered the distance by train and were cosmetically muddied after they had been unloaded, and the first machine home, a Duryea, was not one of the marques under Lawson's aegis (he had expensively purchased a great number of motor car patents in a forlorn effort to monopolize the nascent British car industry).

Demand for motor cars was growing steadily during the latter part of the 1890s, and by now the Benz had become the world's most popular car, with the 2000th production vehicle being delivered in 1899. Motoring was still the sport of a few rich eccentrics, however, and many people had never seen a car.

It was to remedy this defect that, in 1900, the Automobile Club of Great Britain and Ireland held its famous 1000 Miles Trial, which took in most of the major cities of England and Scotland. A total of 65 cars, many English Daimler and MMC models built by Lawson's empire, set out from Hyde Park Corner, London, in April; the major part of this entry finished the run without major mishap, proving that the motor car had at last become a reliable—or relatively so—touring vehicle after a century's gestation.

Couched in glowing Victorian prose, this advertisement (**left**) is, in fact, a pastiche conceived for Daimler's 40th anniversary in 1936! Built by a firm once famed for sewing machines and cycles, the 1898 Hurtu (**below**) (whose name did nothing to recommend the marque to timorous English motorists!) is a typical horseless carriage.

Badges and mascots

Radiator badges were the heraldry of the early motor car. Starting as simply makers' plates fixed to the radiator, badges quickly developed into a minor art form. Some badges, indeed, were masterpieces of the enameller's craft; the Invicta was endowed with a polychromatic butterfly badge delicate enough for jewellery. As for mascots, they began as good luck charms like teddy bears tied to the radiator, but soon the techniques of statuary were being employed to produce mascots of real beauty. The Hispano stork and the Rolls-Royce 'Spirit of Ecstasy' became marque symbols, though owners also commissioned individual mascots, like the Wagnerian soprano whose Métallurgique was endowed with a sterling silver Seigfried clad in chain mail.

(1) The Calometer temperature gauge, a popular 1920s accessory, on a 1927 Morris-Cowley. (2) Packard's emblem – 'a pelican in her piety'. (3) A one-off mascot on a Cadillac V-8. (4) The Hotchkiss badge recalls the firm's origin. (5) A 1914 Star 15.9hp. (6) Jaguar's mascot, derived from a sculpture by motoring artist Gordon Crosby. (7) The Armstrong Siddeley sphinx.

1901 to 1914

THE NEW CENTURY was spectacularly ushered in by 'the car of the day after tomorrow', the Mercedes, designed by Daimler's engineer, Wilhelm Maybach. The contract to produce the first batch of 30 cars had been signed within a month of Gottlieb Daimler's death in March 1900. They had been ordered by the wealthy Austro-Hungarian Consul at Nice, Emil Jellinek, who insisted that they be christened after his daughter Mercédès, a name which found such favour with the wealthy car-buying public that all German Daimler cars were soon known as 'Mercedes', too.

The advanced design of the Mercedes, which combined in one harmonious whole elements such as the honeycomb radiator, pressed steel chassis and gear-lever moving in a gate rather than a quadrant, 'set the fashion to the world' and soon many high-priced cars were copying its layout; even comparatively small cars like the Peugeot were built on Mercedes lines.

These cars did not, however, represent the 'popular motoring' of the early 1900s; this was the province of single-cylinder runabouts like the De Dion and the Renault—again, these well-built cars were widely imitated—and, in America, first by light and temperamental steam cars like the Locomobile and then by gas buggies, of which the most famous was the Curved-Dash Oldsmobile.

But the development of the motor industry in America was being hampered—as it had in Britain a few years earlier—by the shadow of monopoly. A patent lawyer named George Baldwin Selden had drawn up a 'master patent' for the motor vehicle in 1879, published it in 1895 and claimed that all gasoline-driven vehicles were infringements of that patent. His claims were eventually given commercial teeth by the Association of Licenced Automobile Manufacturers, established to administer the Selden Patent in 1902, to which most major American car firms were persuaded to belong.

However, Henry Ford, who founded his Ford Motor Company in June 1903, decided to stand against the ALAM, who began proceedings against him in 1904. After lengthy litigation, which resulted in the ALAM building a car to Selden's 1879 design and Ford building a car with an engine based on that of the 1863 Lenoir, Ford won the day in 1911—not long before the Selden Patent would have expired anyway—but the victory established him as a folk hero.

Ford's great achievement, after five years' work, was to introduce in October 1908 the immortal Model T, which became so popular that he was forced to introduce the car industry's first moving production line in order to build enough cars to satisfy demand. His 'Universal Car' changed the face of motoring; over 16·5 million were built before production ended in 1927, truly 'putting the world on wheels' and transforming the face of society.

A 1901 Curved-Dash Oldsmobile

Though the Edwardian era saw motoring become more popular, on the other hand it also saw the finest and most elegant cars of all time, built to a standard of craftsmanship which could never be repeated. After World War One, many of the great marques faded away in a genteel decline: Delaunay-Belleville, 'the Car Magnificent', the favourite marque of the Tsar of Russia and one of the very best of the French cars of the pre-1914 era, became just a *petit bourgeois* in the 1920s.

Napier, the British company which popularized the six-cylinder engine, enjoyed perhaps even greater acclaim than its rival, Rolls-Royce, while its sales were controlled by that bombastic character Selwyn Francis Edge; when Napier gave him a £160,000 'golden handshake' after a dispute over policy in 1912, however, the company's fortunes seemed to leave with him. Edge, having agreed to leave the motor industry for seven years, became a successful Sussex pig-farmer; Napier built very few cars after the war, concentrating instead on its aero engines.

Such ostentatious machinery relied for its existence on a pool of highly skilled, lowly paid craftsmen with a surpassing pride in their work; against the onslaught of cheap machines produced in America by unskilled labour using production techniques which eliminated most of the human factor, the big luxury cars stood little chance. They represented only a tiny fraction of the potential market for the motor vehicle and, even if their production had not been decimated by the drying up of the car market as a result of the war, they would inevitably have died out as a result of the social changes in the post-war world.

Europe, indeed, experienced an outburst of popular motoring in the 1910–14 period which owed nothing to American concepts of mass production; instead, it grew out of the motor-cycle industry, whose engines, single-cylinder or vee-twin, offered lightness and power. Optimistic enthusiasts installed these engines in chassis of often suicidal crudeness, with cart-type centre-pivot steering in many cases, as well as other unmechanical devices such as wire cables coiled round the steering column instead of a conventional steering box and drag link, belt and pulley transmission and tandem-seat layouts with the driver in the second row of the stalls. These crude devices, known as cyclecars, flourished especially in England and France; attempts to transplant them to America failed because they were simply unsuited to the very different motoring environment there.

The worst of the cyclecars were short-lived, however; the designs of the late Edwardian period which promised perhaps the most for the future were the new light cars like the Morris-Oxford, the Standard and the Hillman, all 'big cars in miniature' of around 1100cc, with four cylinders and built on proper engineering lines. These admirable machines were to be the pattern for the popular family cars of the 1920s.

One of the great names of motoring in the Edwardian era was Napier: this 1907 60hp six-cylinder (**1**) has been constructed as a replica of the car on which S. F. Edge averaged over 60mph for 24 hours to inaugurate the Brooklands race track. This 1903 Fiat 16/20hp (**2**) was shown at the Agricultural Hall Exhibition in London: its Grosvenor tonneau body is English-built. The popular impression that motor cars were 'engines of death' is illustrated by this 1904 cartoon (**3**); a more idealized concept of motoring is shown in the 1908 Argyll advertisement (**4**).

Another, if humbler, 'immortal' of the period was the twin-cylinder Renault AX (**5**), for this chassis was used on the taxis which ferried troops to the Battle of the Marne and saved Paris in 1914. Some of the ignorant fear of motoring may have been caused by the strange garb affected by early motorists, like these sinister anti-dust masks (**6**), from 1907.

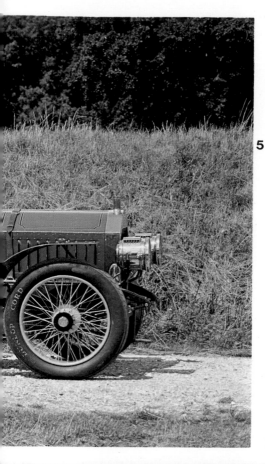

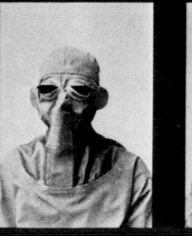

Wheels

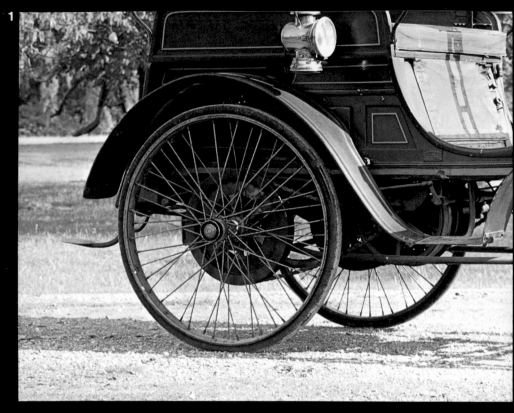

The wheel is one of man's most fundamental inventions, as it has no parallel in nature. The earliest cars rolled into the world on wire wheels derived from cycle practice, or on wooden wheels developed from those used on carriages. These basic types have been followed by many different patterns of wheel: only the roundness has remained constant.

The wire wheels of the 1898 Hurtu (**1**) are typical of those used on many early light cars. Their spindly construction makes them unsuitable for high speed. One of the odder inventions of Edwardian times was this hub-mounted tyre pump (**2**), here fitted to a wooden-wheeled Gladiator. Wooden artillery wheels (**3**) were common on most pre-World War One European cars, and were still being used in America throughout the 1920s. Bugatti's famous spoked aluminium wheels (**4**) were developed for racing use. Cheap to make and light in weight, they could be changed complete with brake drum.

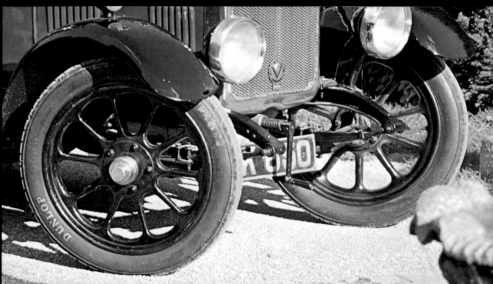

The spokes on the wheels of this Model A Ford (5) are electrically welded to the rim, not located by adjustable nipples as on conventional wire wheels. The wheels on this 1923 Calcott (6) are pressed steel simulating wooden artillery wheels, a popular fashion on British light cars of the 1920s. Wheeltrims have ranged from vulgar (7) to the elegantly practical (8), the latter being used to protect a wire-spoked wheel and make it easier to clean. Styling of wheels is nothing new – compare the Bugatti of the 1930s (9) with the Alfasud (10)

1915 to 1930

THE TECHNOLOGY of the motor age revolutionized the way that World War One was fought. The internal combustion engine gave new mobility to the infantry who, before hostilities in Europe came to a standstill in the trenches, could be rushed to reinforce weak points in the front line (most notably when the French General Gallieni sent 6000 reinforcements to repel Von Kluck's attack on Paris in 1914); it also provided motorcycles for despatch riders, permitted H. G. Wells's forecast of 'land ironclads' to be fulfilled in the angular shapes of the first armoured cars and tanks and, perhaps most significantly, gave warfare a new dimension by taking it into the air.

One way and another, most of those who fought in the war were given an insight into the utility of the motor vehicle, and when peace came many returning soldiers were only too anxious to spend their demobilization pay on a car of their own. The result was a boom such as the motor industry had never known. Especially in Britain and France, the established manufacturers found themselves contending for the favours of the car-buying public with a whole new sub-industry of optimists who, working from inadequate back-street premises, assembled light cars and cyclecars from proprietary components in the hope that they might make their fortunes. Most found only commercial failure, like the British firm who, with the bailiffs mounting a 24-hour watch outside the doors of their London factory, broke an exit through the unguarded rear wall, loaded as much of their machinery as possible on to the finished chassis and drove off to seek new (but unforthcoming) fortune in the Midlands.

If the American industry had already developed to the extent where success in popular car sales would inevitably go to the established big battalions (even Chrysler, founded in 1924, sprang from the established Maxwell-Briscoe grouping), there was still room in Europe for new mass-producers. Most spectacular of these was André Citroën, a former gear manufacturer, who, with the aim of bringing Ford-style mass-production to France, enjoyed an immediate success with his 10 hp launched in 1919. However, the rise of Citroën spelt doom for the dozens of optimistic assemblers who clustered most thickly in the north-western suburbs of Paris.

The boom collapsed in 1920–21, speeded on its way by strikes, hold-ups, shortages, loss of stock market confidence in the car industry, restrictions on hire-purchase sales, costlier raw materials, and the introduction of a swingeing horsepower tax in Britain.

Only the fittest survived: Ford, whose example was followed by a number of American and European makers, cut prices in order to boost falling sales (though he compensated for

The Blackhawk of 1929 was a short-lived attempt by Stutz to build a lower-priced car.

the loss on the cars by compelling the dealers to take $40-worth of spare parts on which there had been no reduction) and gained a brief respite, though even he had to close down for some months to clear unsold stocks. It was not until 1922 that the motor industry was back on course and a second generation of post-war popular cars began to emerge, most notably the Austin Seven.

Many of the cars of the 1920s profited from the technology of the aero engines developed during the war, most notably the overhead camshaft Hispano-Suiza V-8. Wolseley built this engine under licence and used an overhead camshaft on their post-war cars, but it was not until after the 1927 takeover by Morris that this Wolseley design realized its full potential, especially in MG sports cars.

Hispano-Suiza put their aero engine expertise to full account in the 1919 32cv of 6·6 litres, a splendid machine with servo-assisted four-wheel brakes and delightful handling characteristics, whose overall conception was several years ahead of any of its rivals.

Bentley, who had built rotary aero engines during the war, brought out an in-line four with an overhead camshaft in 1919 (though it was not put into production until 1921); this 3-litre was to become one of the immortal sporting cars.

Many leading manufacturers adopted the overhead camshaft layout during this period, but Rolls-Royce, whose aero engines had used this layout, stuck resolutely to side valves on their cars until the advent of the 20 in 1922; this had pushrod ohv, a configuration followed on the 1925 Phantom which was to supplant the Silver Ghost, which had side valves till the end.

Oddly enough, apart from honourable exceptions like the Hispano, it was the cheaper cars which pioneered the use of brakes on all four wheels, one of the most positive advances in car equipment in the early 1920s. Possibly it was felt that luxury cars would be handled by professional drivers, who would be less likely to indulge in the kind of reckless driving that would require powerful brakes! Moreover, some American popular car makers, appalled at the cost of retooling their cars to accept brakes on the front wheels, actually campaigned against their introduction on the grounds that they were dangerous.

As the decade wore on, more features designed to make motoring more comfortable and safer became commonplace—windscreen wipers, electric starters, safety glass (first standardized on the 1928 Model A Ford), all-steel coachwork, saloon bodies, low-pressure tyres, cellulose paint and chromium plating all became available on popular cars. Styling and the annual model change became an accepted part of the selling of motor cars, bringing with them huge tooling costs which could only be borne by the biggest companies. Many old-established firms just could not keep up and were swept away by the onslaught of the depression in 1929.

Typical of American quality car design in the late 1920s is this 1929 Packard 640 six-cylinder phaeton (**1**). The Hispano H6B (**2**) was one of the great designs of the 1920s. A 1925 aluminium-bodied sports version of the 10.8hp Riley (**3**), normally known as the 'Redwinger'. Two of the most famous popular cars of the era were the Morris-Cowley 'Bullnose' (**4**) and the Model T Ford (**5**). Their very different designs reflect popular taste in Britain and America.

Body styles

1

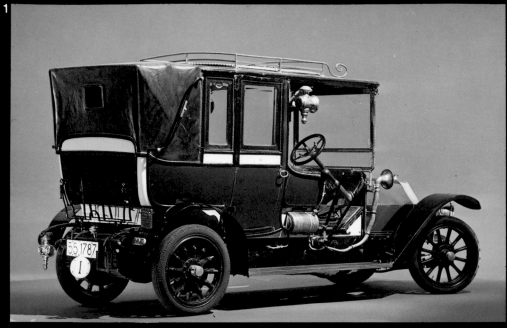

Since the dawn of motoring, a bewildering lexicon of words has been used to describe automobile bodywork, many descending from horse-carriage practice, others coined by car manufacturers. Some became standard practice, like the use of the word 'torpedo' to describe an open four-seater touring car; others, like the similar 'gunboat roadster', vanished into limbo. Fashion, too, has played its part in determining names: in America, 'touring' was superseded by 'phaeton' in an attempt to standardize coachwork nomenclature. And, of course, there are the national differences in usage – a 'saloon' is a closed car in England, a public bar in America, where the car becomes a 'sedan'. Henry Ford devised the names 'Tudor' (two-door) and 'Fordor' (four-door) to describe the Model T sedan; after more than 50 years these names are still in use internally in the Ford Motor Company. Today, there is little variation in body styles – most cars are saloons, though 'hatchback' and 'notchback' are specialized subdivisions of the type. Legislation has all but killed off the convertible, save for specialist sports cars, and the word coupé – once used for two-seaters with a folding hood that was normally kept erected – now means any sporting saloon that is lower than average!

2

The pane of glass ahead of the folding rear roof section of this Fiat Tipo 4 (**1**) of *c*.1914 vintage identifies it as a three-quarter landaulette: a landaulette has the rear roof folding from immediately behind the door pillar. A sedan (**2**) of the traditional pattern is mounted on this 1931 Chevrolet. Chrysler, however, created a new name when they applied wood to the metal panelling of their Town and Country range: this 1949 two-seater (**3**) emphasizes the 'sporty-formal' ethos of that model. Designed to eliminate body rattles, the Weymann saloon (**4**), here mounted on a Peugeot, had lightweight wood framing with a leathercloth covering.

3

8

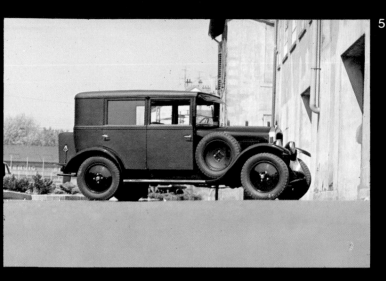

Two-seaters of a semi-sporting nature,
like this 1938 Citroën 7cv (**5**), are often known as
roadsters. The 1975 Lotus Elite (**6**) and the wicker-
bodied Bugatti (**7**) show how specialist
manufacturers are free of the styling constraints
imposed on mass-producers. John Tjaarda styled
the 1937 Lincoln-Zephyr V12 (**8**), one of the
pioneering aerodynamic cars.

1931 to 1945

PERHAPS THE MOST significant pointer to the changing status of the motor car can be gauged from the fact that, at the beginning of the 1920s, the majority of cars were open tourers; by 1931, saloon bodies were fitted to 90 per cent of the cars produced. A contemporary editorial sums up the more functional, utilitarian role of the typical 1930s motor car: 'Today there is no room for the cheap and shoddy, or for immature design. The day has passed when unmechanical contraptions can claim the serious attention of the public... manufacturers no longer expect the public to carry out the testing of new productions for them'.

However, the public was also calling for smaller engines, more suited to the economic climate of the times. To cope with the weight of saloon bodywork and all the popular accessories, these little engines had to be geared low. Consequently they revved high and hard, and their bores wore alarmingly. The days when durability was a feature taken for granted on all but the shoddiest of cars seemed long past.

The design of cars now began to change radically as well. The demand for more capacious bodywork on small chassis led to the engine being pushed forward over the front axle. The radiator became a functional unit concealed behind a decorative grille which became more elaborate and exaggerated as the decade wore on until on some cars it resembled a chromium-plated waterfall or fencer's mask.

During the 1930–35 period, there was a vogue for streamlining which found its full flower in devices like the Chrysler Airflow, the Singer Airstream and the Fitzmaurice-bodied Ford V-8. Even on more staid cars, the angularity of line that had characterized the models of the late 1920s gave way to more flowing contours. Though most cars still retained running boards, the separate side valances were eliminated by bringing the lower door edges down to give a lower, more bulbous look, accentuated by the adoption of wings with side panels, often blended into the radiator and bonnet.

The swept tails of the new-style coachwork now usually concealed some kind of luggage accommodation as well, a feature sadly lacking on most 1920s models, which usually boasted a luggage grid and nothing more.

'Well-rounded and commodious', the cars of the 1930s offered greater comfort and convenience than their forebears. The stylist, however, had taken over from the engineer and the craftsman bodybuilder and, as a result, the new cars were often deficient in handling as the main masses were now concentrated at either end, like a dumb-bell. New suspension systems— especially independent front springing—also brought their handling problems, and some cars had to be fitted with bumpers incorporating a harmonic damping device to prevent them from

Henry Ford's 'last mechanical triumph' was his 1932 V8, seen here with phaeton bodywork.

shimmying right off the road on their supersoft springing.

Not that all was gloom and despondency in the 1930s: some manufacturers produced excellent cars during the decade. Morris and Austin continued to build soundly engineered small cars (though Herbert Austin was distinctly upset when his designers insisted on moving the radiator behind a dummy grille, as he felt that it was a kind of heresy), while the last two new models in which Henry Ford was personally involved, the 8hp Model 19Y and the V-8 (both appeared in 1932), were instantly and deservedly successful.

And, of course, there was the famous front-wheel-drive Citroën, which made its debut in 1934. Though its development costs had all but bankrupted André Citroën—who was forced to sell out to Michelin—this was one of the truly great cars.

A lesser, though no less significant, happening was the metamorphosis of the SS marque from a merely meretricious styling exercise into a modestly priced, excellently finished, well-equipped saloon—the first Jaguar.

The same year that the SS Jaguar was launched—1936—Dr Porsche built the prototype Volkswagens, the 'Strength through Joy' cars sponsored by the Nazi Party and intended to be sold to the German public at £50–£55 to keep them from buying imported models—the first of over 20 million of this most popular car of all time. Few Volkswagens, however, were built before the war (though the design was readily adapted for military purposes).

In many ways the 1930s were a watershed—they saw the last of the big luxury cars from makers such as Hispano-Suiza, Duesenberg and Minerva, as well as the end of many small, independent manufacturers and coachbuilders (victims of the swing to mass-produced cars with pressed-steel bodies). The motor industry had reached the point where it had become vital to the economic well-being of the major industrialized countries. Now it was to prove just as vital in providing weapons of war.

In Britain, five of the largest motor manufacturers set up 'shadow factories' in the late 1930s which could be used to produce aero engine parts in the event of war—they were to produce many thousands of aero engines and complete aircraft during the hostilities. Ford joined the five soon after the outbreak of war and was soon building Rolls-Royce Merlin engines on a moving production line in Manchester, while in the USA Ford mass-production expertise was given its greatest test in manufacturing Liberator bombers on a gigantic production line at Willow Run, Michigan.

From the ubiquitous Jeep, through staff cars, trucks, tanks and powerboats to the biggest bomber aircraft, the motor industry played a crucial role in World War Two. Re-adapting to peacetime production was, however, to prove almost as big a test of the industry's abilities.

2

3

6

The 1930s saw a rapid evolution in body design, from traditional shapes like the Zagato-bodied 2.3-litre Alfa Romeo (**6**) – which nevertheless influenced the styling of many lesser breeds of sports car – to the avant-garde Cord (**1**) designed by Ray Dietrich and deemed worthy to be shown in New York's Museum of Modern Art. The Type 57 Bugatti (**2**) has saloon coachwork far more restrained than some of Jean Bugatti's creations on this chassis, while patrician marques like Packard (**3**) and Rolls-Royce (**4**) made some concessions to fashion while retaining their innate dignity. So, too, at a more humble level, did the Austin Seven (**5**).

Engines

1

Sophisticated and powerful though the engine of a modern car may be, nevertheless it operates on principles first successfully applied over a century ago. The first car engines were simple affairs, usually with one or two cylinders, though since the turn of the century multi-cylinder power units have predominated, normally with four, six or eight cylinders, though non-conformist configurations with three, five, twelve or sixteen cylinders have been tried. Rotary engines have also made sporadic appearances, too. But the main changes in the power unit have been technical improvements: the replacement of the atmospherically operated automatic inlet valve by mechanical inlet valves in the early 1900s, the adoption of monobloc cylinder castings instead of cylinders cast singly or in pairs, the general use of detachable cylinder heads, and the change from side to overhead valves. Today, the overhead camshaft, once the premise of high-powered sports and racing cars, is a common feature of family cars, thanks to the invention of the cogged driving belt, which replaces the complex gear trains of earlier designs and is cheap to install and silent in operation.

2

3

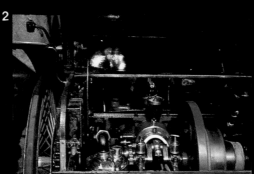

4

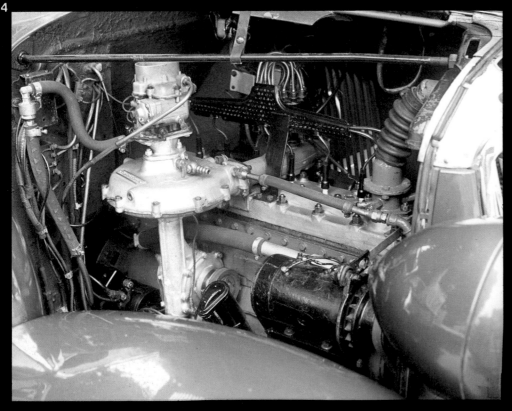

Engines developed rapidly: compare the 1908 Hutton (**1**) with its electrolytically-deposited copper water-jackets and dual ignition (the twin carburettors are an anachronism) with the primitive 1900 Benz (**2**) which has an exposed, grease-lubricated crankshaft like its 1885 forebear. The Jaguar XK120 engine, with its twin ohc (**3**) was a classic 1940s design capable of great development, while the 1934 Graham straight-eight, with its centrifugal supercharger (**4**), was a more short-lived way of obtaining increased performance.

6

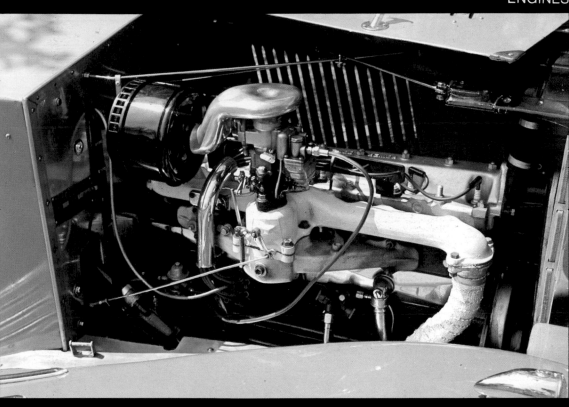

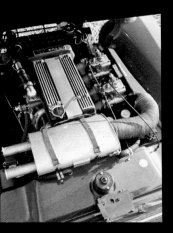

8

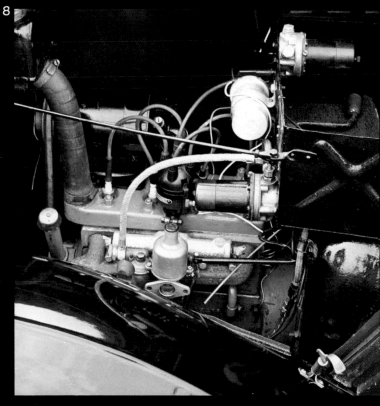

9

A more modestly priced dohc power unit was the Lotus Twin Cam, here seen in a 1971 Lotus Super Seven (**5**), while the Oldsmobile six in this 1936 Railton (**6**) was a simple side-valve unit relying on good power/weight ratio for performance. In more Wagnerian vein is the 1908 Grand Prix Benz unit (**7**), which promised plenty of 'sturm und drang' with pushrod ohv and drainpipe exhaust. Measure it against the tiny sv engine of the 1936 Morris Eight (**8**) and the powerful American Ford V-8 of the 1970 AC Cobra (**9**).

1946 to 1960

BESET BY POST-WAR materials shortages and government interference, motor manufacturers nevertheless soon returned to production, inevitably with slightly modernized pre-war models in most cases though some manufacturers did actually manage to produce all-new cars, notably Armstrong-Siddeley in Britain.

Despite shortages of fuel and tyres, there was a vast demand in Britain for cars, but the government forced manufacturers to export half their output, even though these cars had been designed mostly for the very insular requirements of pre-war Britain. To curb the speculators who had been buying new cars and selling them at an inflated profit, purchasers had to sign a 'covenant' guaranteeing that they would not resell for initially one year, later two.

There was much talk of technical developments arising from wartime projects, but devices such as automatic transmission were only generally adopted in America, and reports that hydraulic suspension, or springing by rubber or torsion bars, were about to be adopted on British cars proved to be more than a little premature. Indeed, some makers seemed unready to come to terms with the future, as one report noted: 'Since wind resistance is an important factor in brake performance, streamlining may lead to braking difficulties, as was shown in experiments carried out in France'.

European manufacturers had also the problem of rebuilding war-shattered plant; in France, the industry had lost machine tools, equipment and labour to Germany and suffered much bomb damage. A shortage of sheet steel and tyres also helped to keep production to about a sixth of the 1938 level in 1946–48, though some recovery was apparent by 1949 when the first post-war Salon de l'Automobile was held in Paris and production had risen to about four times the 1938 monthly level.

Other manufacturing countries had similar difficulties, those of Germany being compounded by the division of the country and the replacement of the Reichsmark (£1 = RM24) by the Deutschmark (£1 = DM11.75), an effective devaluation of around 100 per cent. Nevertheless, the country's most prolific manufacturer, Volkswagen, continued to make progress despite opinions from British experts—and from Henry Ford II—that the VW was too noisy and uncomfortable to be competitive. And though the BMW factory had ended up in the Russian Zone, the first—and only—'war reparation' design to come out of Germany became the BMW-based Bristol 400.

That was only one of the classic sports cars to appear after the war; more famous still was the Jaguar XK 120, with a twin-cam engine reportedly developed during wartime firewatching duty. It made its debut in 1948 along with two, more utilitarian, designs — the Morris Minor and the Citroën 2 cv.

A classic post-war sports car, the Jaguar XK 120

Built by the most traditionally minded motor company of all, the Morgan 4/4 (**1**) of the 1950s was little changed in appearance from its ancestor of the mid-1930s. Like all Morgans built since 1910, it had sliding-pillar independent front suspension. The advanced and complex Citroën DS (**2**) supplanted the immortal *traction avant* in 1955. The 1946 Lincoln (**3**) shows how even quality post-war American cars adopted extreme styling for their radiator grilles.

The 1950s saw the motor industry entering a period of traumatic change. Those brave attempts by independent companies like Kaiser and Crosley to carve a foothold in the American market against the corporate giants of the Big Three—Ford, GM and Chrysler—came to nothing, and the most respected of the old-established independents like Packard, Nash and Studebaker were in decline and would soon vanish, either by attrition or by merger. The American car industry had become stereotyped. Its typical product—generally superlatively hideous—had either a six-cylinder engine (often of fairly antique provenance) or a V-8, and boasted excruciatingly named accessories and components like Hi-Fyre or Firedome engines, HydraMatic or UltraMatic transmissions, even FlightSweep styling. This was the era of the exaggerated tailfin and the grinning chrome grille, and the 'performance car' that could only go fast in a straight line. The announcement of small 'compact' cars in 1959 brought, as well as the Ford Falcon and Chrysler Valiant of conventional design, the unorthodox rear-engined Chevrolet Corvair whose unAmerican handling activities ensured that the US industry went straight from nadir to Nader.

There were mergers in Europe, too, like the shotgun wedding between Austin and Morris, a union born out of strife which would lay the seeds of trouble for that British Motor Corporation's ultimate descendant, British Leyland. But, at that time, their products—small family cars—were just what the public wanted. Fuel economy became even more significant after the 1956 Suez War, when petrol was rationed, and the event created a new race of cyclecars, only now they called them 'bubblecars', and many of them came from German firms grounded in the aircraft industry like Heinkel and Messerschmitt.

In the main, these bubblecars were beastly machines whose only merit lay in their economy; their death-knell was tolled by the advent of an epochal design by Alec Issigonis—the 1959 Mini Minor, which gave a new word to the popular vocabulary and heralded a new race of decently engineered small cars with sports car-like handling. Its layout of front-wheel drive and transverse engine was to set the pattern for the coming 20 years and more.

But the 1950s had their glamour cars, too: Britain produced the big Healeys, the Triumph TRs and the first MG to abandon the perpendicular lines of the 1930s, the slippery profiled MGA, even available with a temperamental twin-cam engine; Italy built big, powerful sports cars like the Ferrari America and Super America; France, which had taxed the *grand'routiers* like Delahaye out of existence, introduced the avant-garde Citroën DS; and Germany, once again *persona grata* after its post-war isolation, brought out the unique and distinctive Mercedes 300SL coupé, with its stylish, if not entirely practical, gull-wing doors.

One of the most sought-after sports cars of the 1950s, both then and now, was the 300SL Mercedes (4), with its unorthodox gull-wing doors. Cadillac set the fashion for fins in the 1950s: by the 1954 models (5) this vulgar trend had reached its peak.

5

Dashboards

Though the very first cars were devoid of instruments, by 1899 enterprising accessory manufacturers had begun to offer speedometers: 'motor timepieces' soon followed, along with voltmeters, gradient meters, odometers and petrol gauges. The first 'idiot lights' appeared in 1908 in the shape of a patent oil indicating device which glowed white when there was sufficient oil, red when the level was too low. The invention of the dipstick soon rendered this 'Lubrimeter' superfluous. By 1910, there was even an instrument to measure petrol consumption. Some of these ingenious devices, too far ahead of their time to be commercially viable, have been 're-invented' and, in modern form, appear on some of the latest cars.

Compare the traditional approach of the instrument panel on the 1959 R-type Continental Bentley (1) with the modern approach (2) of the 1979 Saab 900 saloon, with padded steering wheel for safety. The 1951 Porsche 356 Speedster's instrument panel (3) reflects the character both of the car and of the era in which it was built.

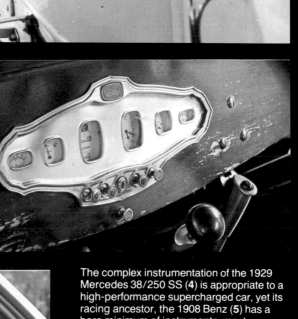

The complex instrumentation of the 1929 Mercedes 38/250 SS (**4**) is appropriate to a high-performance supercharged car, yet its racing ancestor, the 1908 Benz (**5**) has a bare minimum of instruments, most importantly the drip indicator which shows that oil is going to the engine bearings in sufficient quantity. The 1979 Panther J72 (**6**) represents an attempt to blend traditional dash layout with modern safety requirements. In late-1920s American cars, like the 1929 Stutz Blackhawk (**7**), the hand of the stylist appeared to be set against easy interpretation of the instrument readings, a defect shared by the 1958 Chevrolet dash (**8**). The 1979 Aston Martin (**9**), however, represents a return to classicism (though its stablemate, the Lagonda, made extensive use of digital readouts).

1961 to 1979

THE VERY SUCCESS of the American compact cars brought new problems to their makers in the early 1960s. For, instead of capturing a whole new market, they encroached into established sales areas, and American dealers began the decade with upwards of a million unsold 'full-size' cars on their hands. Not only that, but the compacts also hit exports of European cars to the USA, and many dealers just stopped selling foreign cars. The only two makes which really managed to hang on to their American sales were Volkswagen and Renault; interestingly enough, in the late 1970s these two firms were to remain most heavily committed to the USA market, VW opening a plant in Pennsylvania in 1978 which gave them third place in sales in a remarkably short space of time, and Renault tying up a sales deal with AMC (which VW had pushed into fourth place).

America was making its presence felt in Europe, too. Ford of America took control of its English affiliate for a record sum of money, and Chrysler began a step-by-step takeover of the Rootes Group with governmental blessing, the task of sorting out the company's financial problems having been judged beyond the powers of mere government officials.

Mergers were the order of the day, for Standard-Triumph joined up with the Leyland Group in 1960, and the same year Jaguar and Daimler combined. Jaguar-Daimler was itself absorbed by the BMC in 1966, while Leyland took over Rover (which had acquired Alvis). Finally, Leyland and the BMC merged early in 1967, after much hard bargaining (though as a prime reason for the merger had been political rather than commercial, the huge and complex group faced extraordinary difficulties right from the start). The result was British Leyland, which later became BL. The problems it inherited included model lines which competed with one another, thus reducing group efficiency, and the fact that their most outstanding popular model, the Mini, was being produced at a loss—indeed, it was to reach its twentieth birthday before it showed a profit.

German manufacturers were uniting, too: Mercedes had already linked with Auto-Union-DKW, and Volkswagen and NSU also became part of the same grouping during the decade, while the old two-stroke DKW was succeeded by a revived Audi marque. In France, Citroën took over Panhard, one of the industry's oldest marques, in 1965, but ended car production there two years later.

There were many reasons why Europe's manufacturers were joining together—as well as direct mergers, the decade also saw the start of programmes of cooperation jointly to develop components such as engines for the benefit of several makers, who perhaps could

Named after Enzo Ferrari's dead son, the Dino brought Ferrari-style motoring to a wider circle. This is a 1972 model.

not stand the ever-increasing cost of developing new power plants on their own.

And there was a new source of competition as well, for the Japanese were beginning to send their cars to Europe in small numbers. It was the start of an onslaught which was to become such a torrent that, in little over a decade, manufacturers from some European countries—especially Britain—had to strike a 'gentleman's agreement' with the Japanese manufacturers that the latter would hold down exports to a 'prudent' level, since it was felt that their products were placing too much stress on the indigenous manufacturers. Just how good the Japanese products had become was to be emphasized in 1979, when BL announced that it was to build a Honda model as a stopgap.

A crucial turning point in the history of the automobile came with the Arab embargo on oil exports following the Arab-Israeli War of late 1973. Though supplies were gradually restored to something approaching normality, the system had suffered a shock from which it would perhaps never fully recover, for the era of cheap oil was over.

For America, the experience was particularly traumatic, for the public had become accustomed to unlimited use of big, 'gas-guzzling' cars. Shortages in petrol supply gave Americans a chilling reminder of what life without cars could mean. The eventual result, once panic measures like the virtually overnight switching of production from large models to compacts had subsided, was an almost nationwide blanket speed limit of 55 mph and government insistence on the production of more fuel-efficient cars for the 1980s. There was even, following post-revolutionary cuts in petrol supplies from Iran, the introduction in 1979 of rationing in California, where three-car families were common. This represented a dramatic turnabout in future model policies, and involved vast expenditure. For Ford in 1978, the outlay needed to develop new, more economical cars for the early 1980s fuel consumption limits was greater than the total sum of investment over the company's previous 75 years. For General Motors, it represented an annual bill of $3·2 billion from 1975 on to revise its model range, an increase of 135 per cent on previous years. And for Chrysler, finance had to be found by selling off most of its foreign holdings, notably Chrysler Europe, acquired by Peugeot-Citroën.

In fact, Europe was now the focus of the world car industry. The European manufacturers had overtaken the output of American firms in the late 1960s, and, by the end of the 1970s, were building about 20 per cent more. Long conditioned by higher petrol prices and fiscal restrictions on engine size, Europe had developed smaller, more efficient cars.

In less than a century, the motor car has totally changed society, and become vital to the economic life of many nations. But what does the next century hold for the motor car?

A group of cars which epitomizes the face of motoring in the 1970s. The 1978 Chrysler (now Talbot) Sunbeam (**1**) is typical of the modern breed of small hatchback cars. Porsche's 928 (**2**) is one of the ultimate sporting cars, while the Range Rover (**3**), with its go-anywhere four-wheel drive, is a practical workhorse as well as a status symbol leisure vehicle. Oldsmobile's Omega (**4**) is one of their 1980 'X-cars', designed to incorporate more 'European' characteristics than earlier American models. Aston Martin's 1979 V8 (**5**) and the Bertone-styled Fiat X1/9 (**6**) show opposite ends of the sporting scale.

Art and the automobile

Since automobile art first arose in Paris at the turn of the century, mainly taking the form of caricatures and allegorical posters, it has embraced many forms and schools of art, being particularly evident in the contemporary Pop Art and Photo Realism movements in the USA. Popular items for collectors of 'automobiliana' include posters, sculptures, mascots, ornaments, glassware, even 'polychrome sculptural masses' formed from car components fed into a hydraulic press.

An 1898 poster (**1**) by Belgian racing cyclist Georges Gaudy, this was one of the first posters to advertise a motor race; the car is probably a Benz, and the driver, Old Father Time. More serious artists are painting car subjects today than at any time in the past, and nowhere is this more evident than in the Pop Art and Photo Realism movements; this example of the Photo Realism school is *Wrecking Yard III* (**2**) by the American Don Eddy. (**3**) A squared-up drawing and water-colour by Geo Ham (Georges Hamel), a famous French illustrator most active in the 1930s and 1940s.

The Michelin Tyre Company's building in Fulham Road, London, was the work of architect François Espinasse. Dating from 1910, it is decorated with coloured tiles depicting contemporary racing successes; this scene (4) is of the 1907 French Grand Prix. The Hispano-Suiza catalogue (5) was illustrated by René Vincent, a leading motoring artist from before World War One to the 1930s. (6) Motoring ornaments are widely collected items of 'automobiliana'; this is a porcelain Art Deco example. *Automobilia* (7) is a 1960s Pop Art composition by Peter Philips. (8) A 3.5-litre BMW decorated by American sculptor Alexander Calder, inventor of the 'mobile'.

The evolution of mass production

THE PHENOMENAL GROWTH of the car industry would not have been possible without the introduction of mass-production methods. It is generally thought that mass production was invented by Henry Ford, and introduced in his Highland Park, Detroit, factory in 1913. Yet Ford was only applying the lessons of over 100 years' progress in large-scale manufacturing.

As far back as 1798, Eli Whitney, given a rush order for 10,000 muskets by the United States Government, built machines that duplicated gun parts so accurately that they could quickly be assembled into finished muskets without hand fitting. He demonstrated this by scrambling the parts of 10 muskets and then assembling a musket from parts taken at random.

Contemporaneously, Marc Brunel (father of Isambard Kingdom Brunel) was supplying the British Navy with rigging blocks produced on automatic machines at Portsmouth Dockyard—'machinery so perfect appears to act with the happy certainty of instinct, and the foresight of reason combined', wrote one visitor. The machines were produced in association with Henry Maudslay, whose standardization of screw threads and accurate lathes and planing machinery brought the standards of precision that would make mass production truly feasible.

Another vital feature of mass production, the moving conveyor belt, had appeared in 1783 in an automatic grain mill devised by Oliver Evans, who later built one of America's first

Today, mass-production car factories are making increasing use of computers to control production processes, as in the Fiat works (**below**). However, there has also been a revival in 'traditional' hand production methods for limited-production cars, as in the Panther factory (**bottom and below right**).

steam carriages. Evans's mill used belt, bucket and screw conveyors, and could be operated by only two men, one pouring grain into a hopper at one end of the mill, the other putting flour into sacks at the other end.

The technique was carried a stage further in the Chicago meat factories from the 1860s, when the meat packers adopted the method of hanging pigs from an overhead conveyor, so that all the operations from slaughtering to jointing were carried out by a series of workers, each carrying out a single operation on the carcass. It took just four minutes from catching a pig in the stock pen until its carcass arrived in the cooling room to be turned into hams, sausages and pork chops. Output was more than doubled.

The idea that output could be multiplied by dividing work had been given impetus by Elihu Root, who joined Samuel Colt's armament factory in 1849 and boosted production of Colt Six Shooters by dividing and simplifying the steps in their manufacture and inventing new machinery to fill the gaps in the sequence.

Frederick Winslow Taylor, a contemporary of Henry Ford, was the original 'efficiency expert', who devised time and motion studies based on the theory that production was fastest when worker efficiency was highest.

Such ideas were more likely to find a receptive audience in America, where skilled labour was scarce and expensive, and American metal-working machinery had become the best in the world by the dawn of the motor age. The Lanchester brothers in Britain were thought remarkable for insisting on rigorous inter-changeability of parts; in America, inter-changeability was a necessity, though men like Henry Leland, schooled in the high standards of

the arms industry, did bring it to a high pitch.

But all the early American mass-production motor manufacturers worked in similar ways: chassis were erected where they stood, parts being brought to them. It worked well enough in industries like the manufacture of sewing machines or typewriters (where America also excelled) but was clumsy where cars were being made in great numbers.

Progress towards more effective production was rapid. White, for example, had an overhead craneway running the full 600ft length of their Cleveland plant, feeding the buildings branching off on either side (though a similar scheme had been used by J. G. Bodmer in England in 1839). Chalmers-Detroit had a chassis assembly room by 1909 in which frames were ranged in two parallel rows, with overhead tracks bringing in motors and other heavy parts at the appropriate moment.

But mass production as we know it today resulted from Henry Ford's combining all the best features of these pioneering ventures in his newly completed Highland Park plant in Detroit in 1913. Ford constantly experimented with gravity slides, conveyors, and the placement of men and tools for maximum efficiency. Breaking each manufacturing operation into its constituent parts, he multiplied the production of anything from flywheel magnetos to complete engines, often by a factor of four.

Department by department he established sub-assembly lines until, in his own words, 'everything in the plant moved'.

The ultimate step was the creation of the moving final assembly line, where the chassis itself moved, starting without wheels at one end of the line and emerging at the other end as a completed car, driven off under its own power.

One of the first Ford components to be mass produced was the flywheel magneto (**right**). This remarkable series of photographs was taken in the Ford Highland Park plant in 1915 to illustrate the first-ever book on mass-production of motor vehicles. Carefully synchronized feeder lines supplied components to the final assembly line, and the mass-production thus made possible enabled prices to be cut and, simultaneously, the minimum daily wage at Ford to be raised to $5. Model Ts came forth in ever-increasing numbers at ever-decreasing prices until a car was leaving the production lines every 10 seconds, at prices as low as $260 (around £50), and an annual production figure of 2,000,000 was achieved.

How cars are made

THE BUILDING OF A CAR begins with the manufacture of its individual components—up to 15,000 of them. Some of the steel components are forged or cast, but most are made from sheet steel pressed into hundreds of different shapes by huge presses capable of exerting pressures of up to 2000 tons per square inch.

The pressings are carried by fork-lift trucks to the pre-production line workshops, and in separate processes the building of the superstructure and underbody begins. First, small sub-assemblies are put together by spot welding. Then these are fitted into jigs, which hold the pieces in place as they are joined by automatic welders; from these the major superstructure and underbody emerge complete. Modern body

weld units can complete up to 1000 welds simultaneously with absolute accuracy.

Now the doors, plus bonnet and boot lid—all arriving ready-made by overhead monorail conveyor—are fitted. Major panel joints have been gas-welded to give greater strength and flexibility when the car is under stress from cornering or rough roads. Finally the bodywork is prepared for painting; each body shell will be finished in plain or metallic colours to an individual order tapped out by teleprinter.

The car is degreased by high-pressure sprays and phosphated to provide a good anti-corrosion and paint adhesion surface; the body is then stoved. Now the car is totally immersed in an electrocoat primer paint process. This

provides a paint film on all areas of the body, including those box sections which are in-accessible under normal processes. The surplus paint is rinsed off and the body is stoved in a gas-fired oven. All outer joints are sealed before the body passes through electrostatic paint spraying equipment. This automatically applies a grey primer sealing coat, which is then stoved. A protective material is applied to the underbody. Each body is wet sanded, rinsed with de-mineralized water and finally dried. The car is then ready to receive three top coats of enamel paint which is applied manually and stoved in a steam-heated oven.

The cars now move on to the trim shop; each has already acquired an individual identity, and

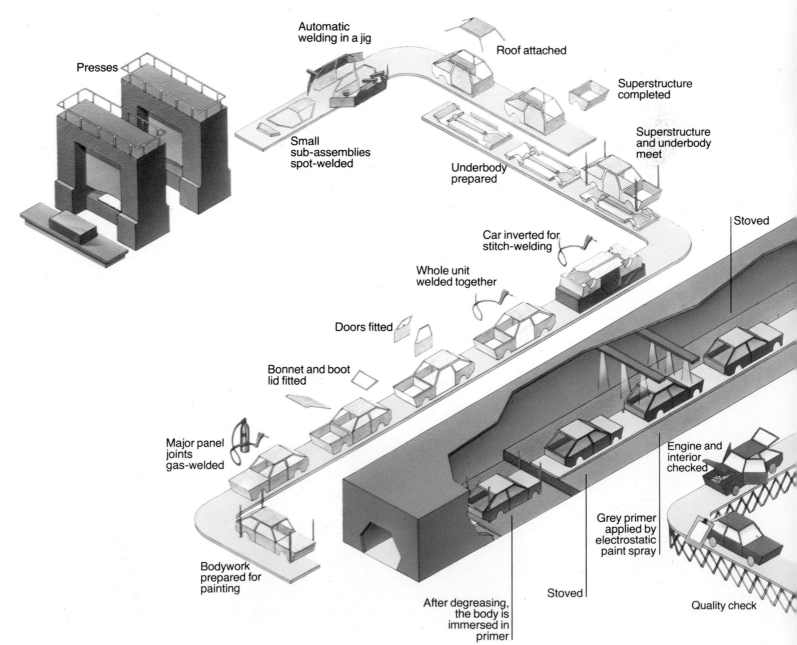

Presses

Automatic welding in a jig

Roof attached

Superstructure completed

Small sub-assemblies spot-welded

Superstructure and underbody meet

Underbody prepared

Stoved

Car inverted for stitch-welding

Whole unit welded together

Doors fitted

Bonnet and boot lid fitted

Engine and interior checked

Major panel joints gas-welded

Grey primer applied by electrostatic paint spray

Bodywork prepared for painting

After degreasing, the body is immersed in primer

Stoved

Quality check

details of its trim specification are transferred from a teleprinter to a card on the bonnet. The build-up starts as components stockpiled beside the production line are fitted—the grille, electrical wiring, lights, head lining, door windows, windscreen.

Then come the under-bonnet parts like horns, battery, brake fluid reservoirs, steering column, radiator and pipes, as well as the instrument panel. Nowadays, much of the complex wiring loom has been eliminated by printed circuits and plug-in modules.

The engine, having been given a 'hot' running test, arrives at the production line complete with carburettors, exhaust manifold, alternator and fan. The clutch/gearbox unit, drive shaft, rear axle, front and rear suspensions—including hubs and brakes—are fitted in a special jig and everything is bolted together. The engine/transmission/suspension assembly moves forward to meet the line from the body shops; the correct body unit is lowered to meet it. The nearly completed car now moves along a raised line. The wipers and interior trim are fitted; the radiator is filled and hydraulic fluid fed into the brake system.

Wheels, made in a separate plant and already fitted with tyres, arrive on a gravity conveyor and are bolted on, and the car rolls forward on its own for the first time. Fuel is added to the tank.

Seats are the last item to be added to the interior. The engine idles as it is checked; then suspension and steering settings are adjusted and checked.

After a final examination of the trim the car undergoes a quality check before it goes on to the roller testing station to test the engine, transmission, steering, brakes and lights. A diagnostic unit checks that the electrical circuit is fully functional. The car is driven on to a conveyorized water test where jets of water at 20 psi are directed on to the cars for four minutes as they pass through the tunnel.

Dried down, it has its final check, then it is parked in the trade compound to await the dealer's delivery conveyor lorries to take it to the showroom.

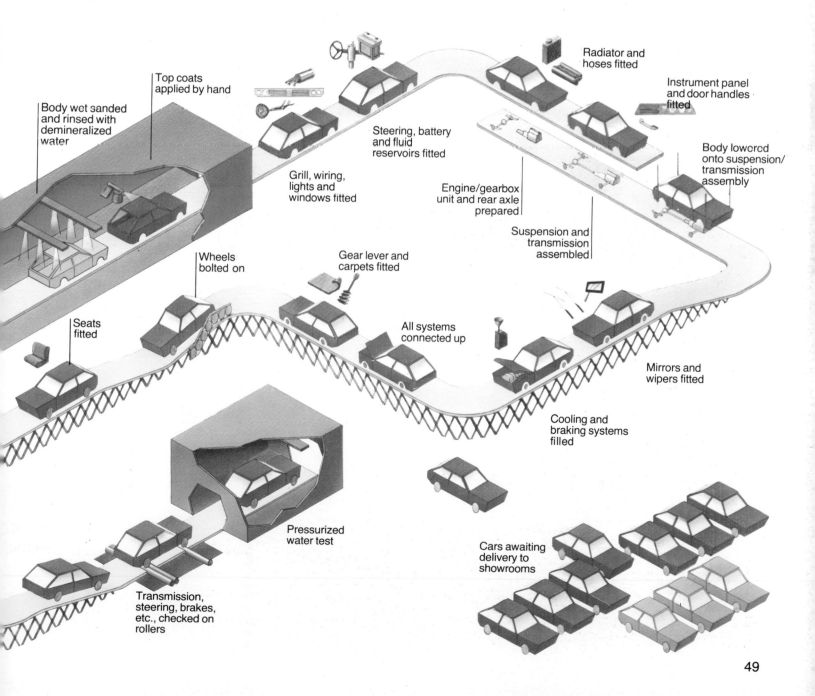

Top coats applied by hand

Body wet sanded and rinsed with demineralized water

Radiator and hoses fitted

Instrument panel and door handles fitted

Steering, battery and fluid reservoirs fitted

Grill, wiring, lights and windows fitted

Engine/gearbox unit and rear axle prepared

Body lowered onto suspension/transmission assembly

Suspension and transmission assembled

Wheels bolted on

Gear lever and carpets fitted

All systems connected up

Mirrors and wipers fitted

Seats fitted

Cooling and braking systems filled

Pressurized water test

Cars awaiting delivery to showrooms

Transmission, steering, brakes, etc., checked on rollers

Developing a new car

A NEW CAR USUALLY starts as a designer's concept, based on a number of assumptions, known as the 'package', which specify the broad outlines of the vehicle—how many passengers the vehicle must accommodate, the layout of engine, transmission and suspension, and the luggage space. Length, width, height, wheelbase and passenger compartment dimensions are also laid down—the cost of developing a new car these days is so great that it must be designed to fill a perceived gap in the market or to succeed a well-established success. Cars are no longer launched in the fond belief that merit alone will sell them.

Each new programme results in a number of sketches for further development, and the best of these are developed into more detailed illustrations—'renderings'—to evaluate the design's potential.

A wheeled 'armature'—a wood and foam plastic skeleton slightly smaller than the finished vehicle—is covered in a special modelling clay, applied warm and shaped to the contours of the design rendering by highly skilled clay modellers. Frequently referring to full-scale brush renderings or fullsize line drawings, the modellers scrape and form the clay using a wide variety of special tools, many of their own manufacture. Because the clay is so malleable, it can be reshaped easily until the designer is satisfied with the appearance of the model.

Now the clay can be 'finished' to give it a realistic appearance. A glossy skin of thin plastic sheet can be applied to simulate paintwork, a similar material gives the impression of windows, and metal foil represents the brightwork.

If the finished clay is approved, a glass-fibre moulding can be taken. This can be fitted with seats, trim and instrument panel (which have already been developed by a separate design team) to give a very good idea of the final form the car will take. Usually, a number of models is made for assessment.

These days, the techniques of the market researcher are often called in to ensure that the production vehicle will appeal to the motoring public. Before one popular model was put into production, the various prototypes were assembled in secret in a hall in Switzerland, and potential buyers flown in from Britain, Germany, Italy, France and Spain to assess these designs and compare them with competitive vehicles. Similar 'clinics' were held in the USA, South America, Spain and Germany. Additionally, surveys questioned over 5000 members of the public on what they expected in terms of engine size, options, specifications and serviceability in such a vehicle. The answers, surprisingly uniform, showed that the designers were on the right track.

During the development stages, a design changes continually, especially now that the

A draughtsman makes a full-size drawing of a proposed new model so that critical dimensions can be evaluated (**left**). Because of the cost of building full-size prototypes, fifth-scale models of a new car are made so that wind-tunnel tests can be carried out to 'fine-tune' the aerodynamics before a project is committed to sheet metal (**above**). Using modelling clay, highly skilled modellers create not only full-size mockups of a new design, but also interior features like the facia panel (**right**).

wind-tunnel is an indispensable part of the design equipment. One family car went through over 250 detail body changes as a result of wind-tunnel testing.

Wind-tunnel testing has produced such features of modern car design as front-end air dams and rear-end spoilers; it has contributed to more economical engines and improved roadholding at speed.

Computers are playing an increased role in car body development, too: the principle is to analyze half of the complete body, which, as the vehicle is virtually symmetrical about a longitudinal centre line, gives information for the whole car.

The input of loads on a vehicle can be computer-simulated, and the computer then caluates the resultant stress distribution throughout the structure. Individual panels can be studied under tension and compression, torsion and bending. Redundant members can be eliminated and panel strengths maximized while still reducing overall weight.

The computer can go beyond designing the basic structure and showing how it will perform in normal service: it can also run crash tests on the theoretical structure. By simulating barrier crash tests on a 'hybrid-analogue' computer, effective 'management' of the energy absorbed in a crash can be arranged. One computer-designed body shell was given an actual crash test when it was found it performed exactly as

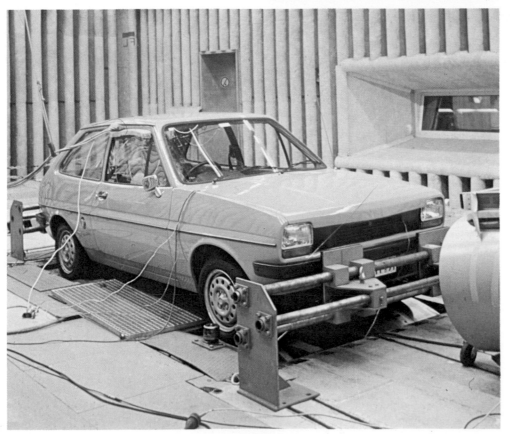

Crash behaviour of new models is assessed in controlled tests (**above**), though today much of the information that used to be gained by destroying expensive prototypes can be gained from computer programmes. Unwanted noises can be detected and eliminated by running tests in an anechoic chamber (**left**), a totally soundless environment. Wind-tunnel tests on the completed prototype (**right**) produce much valuable information.

forecast—the displacement of the steering column into the driving compartment was accurately predicted, and the doors still opened after the impact.

However, computer analysis is only part of the body design process, and must be verified by accelerated tests on the track and in the laboratory. Much valuable time can be saved by simulating the effect of rough roads on a test rig which feeds shock loads into a prototype metal body shell by means of hydraulic rams attached to the suspension pickup points. Tape recordings taken from a test car running across a proving track feed in 'real-life' torsion and bending loads. Finally, prototypes are given extended tests on the manufacturer's proving grounds, where all types of road surface are reproduced and where years of normal use can be condensed into a few weeks.

In fact, before any modern car is put on sale, every component will have been subjected to thousands of test cycles, prototypes will have been deliberately destroyed to prove the protection given by the passenger compartment in accidents, and cost of servicing and maintenance will have been exhaustively analyzed.

The manufacturer will have spent anything up to a billion dollars to develop this new model, and in the end its commercial success or failure still rely on whether the motorist finds it attractive and sound value for money. That is the most crucial test of all.

A global industry

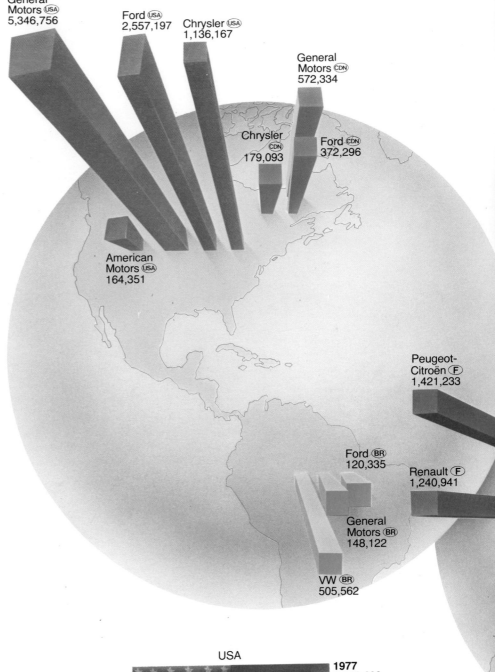

TRADITIONALLY, CAR PRODUCTION has been mainly centred in the northern United States and north-western Europe, with Japan playing an increasingly important role since the 1950s. But now other countries are important car producers. For example, when production of VW's Beetle was phased out in Germany, this robust design continued to be built in Brazil and Nigeria, where its relative simplicity of design made it more suitable for local conditions than more modern and sophisticated designs. And the so-called 'Third World' countries, where labour costs are low, may soon move into world markets as inexorably as the Japanese have done. Already the first South Korean cars have reached Europe, establishing a 'beach-head' for imports from this Asian country whose motor industry is only a few years old (even though, as far back as 1912, it was claimed that the Koreans called all cars 'Ford' because there were so many Model Ts on their roads).

Conversely, the major European and American manufacturers are actively moving into new manufacturing markets, like Egypt, Morocco or Kenya, competing for market supremacy in Mexico, Argentina or Venezuela, and expanding into new European markets like Spain and Portugal.

In the case of the two American giants (Ford and GM), these overseas markets were vital to their continued success in the USA, where a slaving domestic market and the vast expense of meeting the Government's corporate average fuel economy (CAFE) limits meant that, to finance the cars of the 1980s, manufacturers needed the volume that only the world market could supply.

For the third-biggest US company, Chrysler, the cost of meeting CAFE and of developing new models for the 1980s prompted entrenchment and the selling-off of most of its overseas subsidiaries to raise revenue.

Production figures for the principal car manufacturing countries for the years 1947, 1965 and 1977

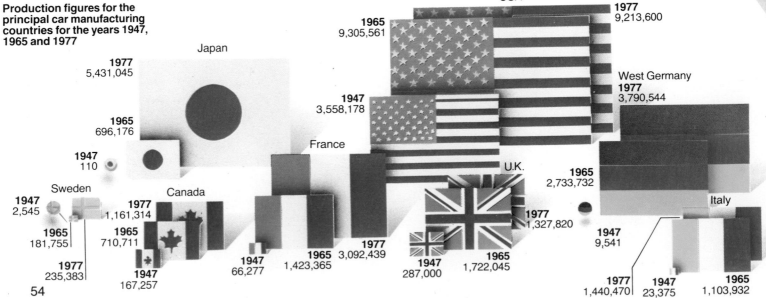

54

**The World's Leading Car
Manufacturers (1978 figures)**

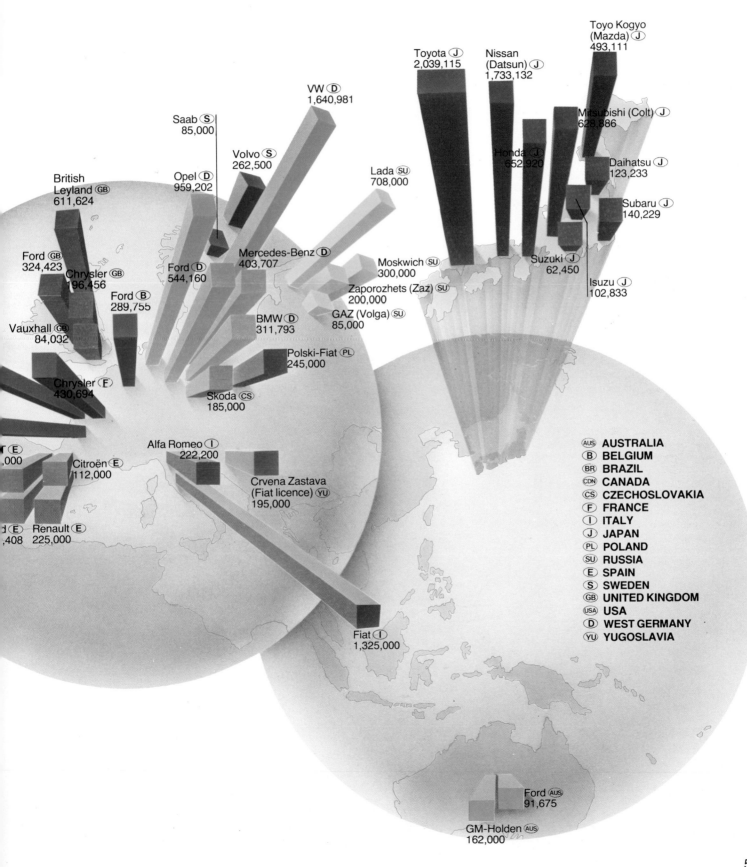

Toyo Kogyo
(Mazda) Ⓙ
493,111

Toyota Ⓙ
2,039,115

Nissan
(Datsun) Ⓙ
1,733,132

Mitsubishi (Colt) Ⓙ
628,886

VW Ⓓ
1,640,981

Saab Ⓢ
85,000

Volvo Ⓢ
262,500

Honda Ⓙ
652,920

Daihatsu Ⓙ
123,233

Opel Ⓓ
959,202

Lada Ⓢⓤ
708,000

British
Leyland ⒼⒷ
611,624

Subaru Ⓙ
140,229

Ford ⒼⒷ
324,423

Chrysler ⒼⒷ
196,456

Ford Ⓓ
544,160

Mercedes-Benz Ⓓ
403,707

Moskwich Ⓢⓤ
300,000

Suzuki Ⓙ
62,450

Isuzu Ⓙ
102,833

Ford Ⓑ
289,755

Zaporozhets (Zaz) Ⓢⓤ
200,000

Vauxhall ⒼⒷ
84,032

BMW Ⓓ
311,793

GAZ (Volga) Ⓢⓤ
85,000

Chrysler Ⓕ
430,694

Polski-Fiat ⓅⓁ
245,000

Skoda ⒸⓈ
185,000

Alfa Romeo Ⓘ
222,200

Ⓔ
,000

Citroën Ⓔ
112,000

Crvena Zastava
(Fiat licence) Ⓨⓤ
195,000

,408   Renault Ⓔ
225,000

Fiat Ⓘ
1,325,000

ⒶⓤⓈ	**AUSTRALIA**
Ⓑ	**BELGIUM**
Ⓑⓡ	**BRAZIL**
ⒸⒹⓃ	**CANADA**
ⒸⓈ	**CZECHOSLOVAKIA**
Ⓕ	**FRANCE**
Ⓘ	**ITALY**
Ⓙ	**JAPAN**
ⓅⓁ	**POLAND**
Ⓢⓤ	**RUSSIA**
Ⓔ	**SPAIN**
Ⓢ	**SWEDEN**
ⒼⒷ	**UNITED KINGDOM**
ⓊⓢⒶ	**USA**
Ⓓ	**WEST GERMANY**
Ⓨⓤ	**YUGOSLAVIA**

Ford ⒶⓤⓈ
91,675

GM-Holden ⒶⓤⓈ
162,000

55

Alternative power sources

THOUGH THE FOUR-STROKE internal combustion engine has been around for over a century, it has had remarkably few challengers to its supremacy.

In the early days of motoring, steam and electricity both had their advocates, but their shortcomings led to their general demise. Steam—external combustion—needed a boiler and water tank, and was complex to operate and maintain, while the electric car needed heavy accumulators to give even the most modest of ranges; it enjoyed something of a vogue in America as a town car, however, up to the 1920s.

Once the electric starter was a commonplace item of equipment, the supremacy of the petrol engine was assured, until, that is, fuel shortages inspired manufacturers to search for viable alternatives. During World War One, cars had been run on coal gas carried in bags like embryo Zeppelins, either on the roof or in trailers; during World War Two, private cars were fitted with gas producers generating combustible gas from carbon, usually in the form of charcoal.

Serious development of alternative power sources did not begin, however, until the 1950s. Rover in Britain led the way with production of gas turbine prototypes, and both General Motors and Ford began experiments along these lines. The major American manufacturers also began looking anew at steam and electric vehicles.

Turbines failed to meet the requirements of the car industry, though they had some attraction to truck builders. Their main fault was a 'time-lag' when accelerating; also, their application to mass-produced cars depends on the development of low-cost, high-temperature components designed for satisfactory engine efficiency and performance.

Another candidate which was tried and found wanting was the Stirling 'hot-air' engine, appropriately designed by a preacher in the early 1800s. Powered by a closed-circuit system utilizing heat expansion of an inert gas, the external-combustion Stirling was at one time seriously considered by Ford as a possibility for the production cars of the late 1980s, but the programme got no further than the building of mobile test beds.

Rotary piston engines, long a fruitful field for hopeful inventors, came to the fore with the Wankel trochoidal engine pioneered by NSU in 1963, but failed to stay the course. Though rotaries are more compact than conventional reciprocating engines, they are costlier to produce and maintain, and are not so fuel-efficient.

Even the 'pollution-free' and noiseless electric car has not solved the problems which bedevilled it at the turn of the century. It still relies on heavy storage batteries with limited range, and needs to be recharged at frequent intervals. And, if its batteries are recharged from a conventional oil-fired generating station, the source of the atmospheric pollution is only

Some modern sports cars, like this 1979 Ford Mustang **(1)**, use an exhaust-driven turbocharger for forced induction to obtain greater efficiency from a conventional petrol engine. In the mid-1960s, Ford of Britain developed a small urban electric car prototype, the Comuta **(2)**, but shelved the project in 1967. The most commercially successful 'alternative' engine is the Wankel rotary-piston unit. This is a Citroën-built example **(3)**. The closed-cycle Ford-Philips Stirling 'hot-air' engine **(4)** was tested in a Pinto car but apparently did not live up to its early promise. In Brazil in 1979, Fiat introduced the 147 saloon running on locally produced sugar cane alcohol **(5)**, promoted by an all-girl rally team. In the summer of 1979, Californian Ken Eacrett drove his solar-powered three-wheeler **(6)** across the USA. Taking its power from a solar panel on the roof, the car had a 25mph top speed.

2

transferred from the car to the power station.

One of the more promising alternative power sources is the stratified-charge engine—basically a more efficient variant of the conventional petrol engine. There are two main types, the divided chamber engine and the fuel-injected stratified-charge engine.

The first type is typified by Honda's CVCC engine, which features a dual carburettor and a precombustion chamber, while Ford's PROCO ('programmed combustion') engine represents the second type. This has a special cylinder and piston head design, and uses fuel injectors to deliver a finely atomized spray of fuel directly into the combustion chamber.

But perhaps the most successful 'alternative engine' is also one of the oldest, the diesel, first devised in the 1890s. Long proven in trucks, by the late 1970s diesels were appearing in a small VW family car, the Golf. Able to run on cheaper, less volatile oil fuel than the petrol engine, and of proven longevity, the compression ignition diesel engine only suffered by comparison, as it tended to be harsher-running and less lively. However, it holds great hope for the future.

Cars of the future

WHAT SHAPE WILL TOMORROW'S car take? One thing is certain: it will not be a science-fiction fantasy vehicle powered by some revolutionary new power plant. Tomorrow's car will, in fact, be very much like today's, except that it will be far more efficient—'socially responsible' is the current in-phrase.

So far, the various alternative power sources that have been tried have all been found wanting: nothing works as well as the internal combustion engine, despite the fact that it has been around for almost a century in production cars. However, it may need to change its diet: petrol is getting scarcer and more expensive, and the prophets of doom say it may run out early in the twenty-first century. Already, new fuels are being investigated. In 1979, Saab-Finland laun-

ched a multifuel engine capable of running on fuel distilled from timber, so that the nation could aim at self-sufficiency.

The US Transportation Secretary Brock Adams called for 'the re-invention of the car', with a target of around 50 miles to the gallon for an American family car of the mid-1980s.

In Sweden, the Royal Academy of Engineering Science forecast that cars of the year 2000, despite the expected stricter anti-pollution and safety requirements, would be as roomy and comfortable as present-day models.

Their equipment, however, will be vastly more sophisticated. Volkswagen—which has declared itself committed to a piston engine for tomorrow's cars—foresees an increased use of electronic aids to driving. In-car computers,

VW predicts, will handle engine management, anti-lock braking, fault diagnosis and crash sensor equipment. By the end of the 1980s, digital displays could have replaced conventional instrument dials, and aircraft-style 'head-up read-outs' will give traffic and weather information from roadside computer links.

More efficient aerodynamics will provide dramatic fuel savings—up to 30 per cent in some cases—and both petrol and diesel engines may be turbocharged for increased efficiency. Low-weight materials will also help fuel economy—Ford-US was already testing carbon-fibre wheels in 1978.

Lighter, quieter, more fuel-efficient, more spacious—these will be the main attributes of tomorrow's car.

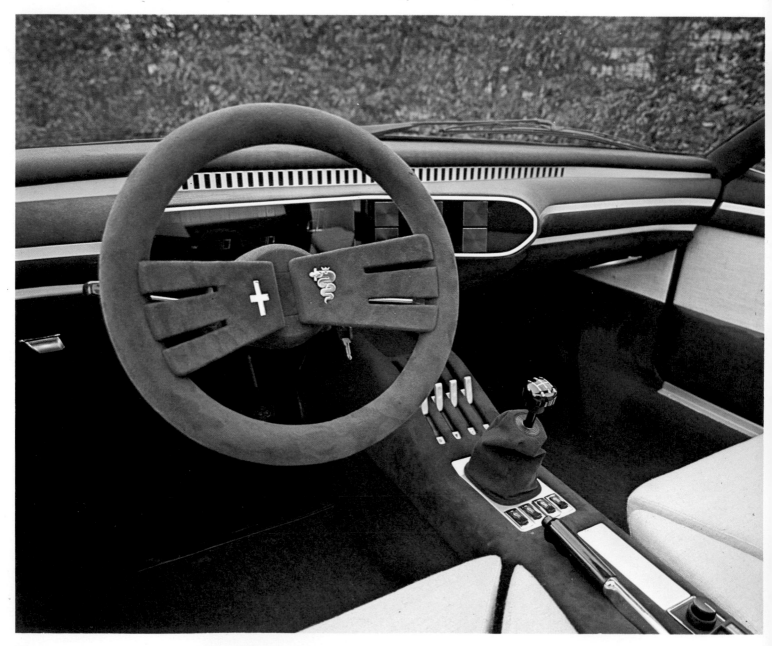

The 'dream cars' of the 1970s take a more thoughtful look into the future than their often bizarre predecessors of the 1950s and 1960s. Aerodynamics play a vital part in their design for an increasingly fuel-conscious world – the Ghia-styled 'Coins' of 1974 (**right**) forecast what shape the Ford sports coupé of the future might take, while the same studio's Corrida (**below**) showed how one car, in this case the Ford Fiesta, could fulfil several functions. Alfa Romeo's Eagle (**opposite**) made interesting use of digital displays instead of conventional instrumentation.

Founders of the motor industry

APPERSON, Edgar *(1870–1959)* **and Elmer** *(1861–1920)*
Collaborated with Elwood Haynes to build one of America's first cars in 1894, later forming Haynes-Apperson. After they broke with Haynes, they founded the Apperson Brothers Motor Car Company.

Herbert Austin

AUSTIN, Herbert *(1866–1941)*
Briton who worked for the Wolseley Sheep Shearing Company in Australia, then returned to England to build the first Wolseley car (1895). Left Wolseley to found Austin (1906), where landmark designs included the Seven and the 12/4. He was knighted in 1917 and became Lord Austin in 1936.

BENTLEY, Walter Owen *(1888–1971)*
Trained as a railway engineer, fitted some of the first aluminium pistons to DFP cars in 1914. After building aeroengines during World War One, he launched the Bentley car in 1919. He later worked for Lagonda.

Karl Benz

BENZ, Karl *(1844–1929)*
Began development of a petrol engine in 1878, founding Benz & Co. in 1883. Built his first motor car in 1885–86, the first petrol car conceived as a unity and owing nothing to horse-drawn carriages.

BIRKIGT, Marc *(1878–1953)*
Swiss engineer who moved to Spain, and became designer of Hispano-Suiza cars and aeroengines.

BOLLEE, Amédée *père* *(1844–1916)*
French bell-founder and designer of steam carriages which pioneered independent front suspension and other technical features well ahead of their time.

BOLLEE, Amédée *fils* *(1867–1926)*
Began with steam carriages, but turned to petrol cars in 1896, building a streamlined racer in 1899 with underslung chassis, rear-mounted twin carburettor, and four-cylinder engine with hemispherical combustion chambers.

BOLLEE, Léon *(1870–1913)*
First achieved fame with the invention of a calculating machine, then, in 1895, devised a sporting tandem-seat voiturette. In contrast, from 1903 he built refined and silent quality cars of advanced design.

BRISCOE, Benjamin *(1869–1945)*
Founded, with Jonathan Maxwell, the Maxwell-Briscoe Motor Company in 1903, and in 1910 organized the United States Motor Company, a combine of some 130 firms, which folded in 1912. In 1913 Briscoe began building cars under his own name. A visit to the 1912 London Motorcycle Show introduced him to cyclecars, which he built in France and America in conjunction with his brother Frank (1875–1954).

BUGATTI, Ettore *(1881–1947)*
Born in Milan, he was designing for De Dietrich before he was 21, moved to Mathis, and in 1910 built the first Bugatti car at Molsheim (Alsace). 'Le Patron', rarely seen without his bowler hat, also affected digitated shoes.

BUICK, David Dunbar *(1855–1929)*
Applied the money he made from the invention of the enamelled bathtub to the development of a car engine with ohv. He then, in 1903, organized the Buick Motor Car Company with backing from the Briscoe brothers, but was bought out by Billy Durant late in 1904.

David Buick

CHADWICK, Lee Sherman *(1875–1958)*
Built his first car in 1899, joining Searchmont in 1900. His Chadwick company lasted from 1903 to 1911, and his racing cars pioneered the use of superchargers. His latter years were spent as the head of a stove company.

CHAPIN, Roy *(1880–1936)*
Started with Olds, then, in 1906, helped found Thomas-Detroit (later Chalmers). In 1909 he organized, along with Howard Coffin, the Hudson Motor Car Company. He was an active crusader for better roads for America.

CHAPMAN, Colin *(born 1928)*
English designer/constructor of Lotus sports and racing cars.

CHARRON, Fernand *(1866–1928)*
French cycle and car racer who collaborated (with Girardot and Voigt) in the CGV car, having made a 'killing' from holding the sole agency for Panhard-Levassor at a time of great demand. Sold his share of Charron Ltd. (as CGV became) to work for his father-in-law, Adolphe Clément, but they split up and Charron eventually built the 'Alda' car. Though he was very bald, the fashionable M. Charron rarely wore a hat, a matter for some comment at the time.

Louis Chevrolet

CHEVROLET, Louis *(1878–1941)*
Swiss racing driver who arrived in the USA in 1900 to sell a wine pump he had invented. He became a team driver for Buick and, with Etienne Planche, designed the first Chevrolet Six in 1911. He left Chevrolet to found the Frontenac Motor Company, building racing cars and 'go-faster' equipment for Model T Fords.

CHRISTIE, John Walter *(1886–1944)*
Pioneered front-wheel drive in the USA, even competing in the French Grand Prix with huge, if not particularly reliable, fwd racers. He also produced fwd tractor units for fire appliances and built an advanced tank in the 1930s.

CHRYSLER, Walter Percy *(1875–1940)*
A locomotive engineer who joined Buick in 1911, rising to become President – as well as first Vice-President of General Motors. Moved to Willys in 1920, saving this company – and Maxwell-Chalmers – from bankruptcy. He converted Maxwell into the Chrysler Corporation, acquiring Dodge in 1928.

CITROEN, André *(1878–1935)*
Frenchman who worked with Mors pre-World War One, and devised a double chevron gear which was used as the emblem of the car-producing company he founded in 1919. Development of a magnificent new factory and of the classic fwd Citroën car caused his death.

CLEMENT, Adolphe *(1855–1928)*
French cycle manufacturer who made a fortune from the French rights for the Dunlop pneumatic tyre and his exceedingly complex business dealings when he entered the motor car industry. As a result of selling the manufacturing rights to the 'Clément' car, he changed his name to 'Clément-Bayard'. His company also pioneered aeroplanes and airships.

COATALEN, Louis *(1879–1962)*
Breton engineer who came to England in 1900, working for Crowden, Humber and Hillman. His greatest designs were for Sunbeam, where he became Managing Director and built the first V-12 racing car in 1913.

CORD, Erret Lobban *(1894–1974)*
Dynamic entrepreneur who created the Auburn-Duesenberg-Cord empire, and also owned Lycoming engines, American Airlines, Stinson Aircraft and New York Shipbuilding before he was 35.

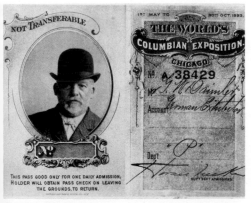

Gottlieb Daimler

DAIMLER, Gottlieb *(1834–1900)*
Born in Württemberg and trained as an engineer; becoming interested in gas engines in the 1860s, he helped develop the Otto gas engine. During the 1880s he set up on his own to develop a 'universal power source' in the shape of a light petrol engine, in collaboration with Wilhelm Maybach. This engine was fitted into a carriage in 1886, creating the first Daimler car.

DARRACQ, Alexandre *(1855–1931)*
Born in Bordeaux, Darracq entered the cycle industry in 1891, building 'Gladiator' cycles;

selling out in 1896, he moved first into components, then into motor vehicles. Darracq voiturettes were particularly famous. He retired in 1912 to take a financial interest in the Deauville casino. Though Darracq built many thousands of cars, he never drove and disliked riding in them.

Georges Bouton (*left*) and Albert De Dion

DE DION, Albert *(1856–1946)*
Famous as a duellist and gambler, Comte De Dion sponsored two brothers-in-law, Bouton and Trépardoux, in the construction of steam carriages. The first practicable De Dion Bouton petrol engines appeared in 1894 and were fitted to tricycles, voiturettes (for which the marque became renowned) appearing in 1899. De Dion also founded the motoring daily *L'Auto*. He became a Marquis in 1901.

DELAGE, Louis *(1877–1947)*
French builder who supplied components to marques such as Helbe, then made complete Delage light cars from 1906. After 1919, Delage also built luxury cars.

DOBLE, Abner *(1890–1961)*
Built his first steam car in 1906, and drove a prototype to Detroit in 1914 to seek backing. Began production in San Francisco in 1920. Output was always limited, but he gained great acclaim. He later acted as a steam power consultant for overseas firms, including Sentinel steam waggons in England.

DODGE, John *(1864–1920)* **and Horace** *(1868–1920)*
Machinists and cycle makers, the Dodges built transmissions for Olds (1901–02), then made chassis and engines for Henry Ford in return for a tenth of his company. They sold their Ford shares for $25,000,000 and founded the Dodge Brothers company, coining the word 'dependable' to describe their products.

DUESENBERG, Frederick *(1877–1932)*
Designed his first car in 1904, and by 1913 had organized the Duesenberg Motor Company to

build engines. During the 1930s Fred and his brother August built the Duesenberg luxury cars, though E. L. Cord took control of the company in 1927. Fred Duesenberg died in a car crash.

DURANT, William Crapo *(1860–1947)*
Having become a major force in the carriage industry, Billy Durant took over Buick in 1904, then, in 1908, founded the General Motors group. Ousted in 1910, by 1915 he was ready to take over again via his Chevrolet company. However, a share crash in 1920 put him out of GM again, so he established a 'Second Empire' which survived until the Depression.

DURYEA, Charles *(1861–1939)* **and Frank** *(1870–1967)*
In 1893 built the first practicable American car to lead to a production company, the Duryea Motor Power Wagon Company (1896).

EARL, Harley *(1893–1969)*
In the early 1920s was a director of Don Lee Corporation, which built custom coachwork for the wealthy. Became director of 'art and color' at GM in 1927, and is recognized as the first mass-production stylist. Among his styling innovations were tailfins.

S. F. Edge on a 1903 Napier

EDGE, Selwyn Francis *(1868–1940)*
Born in Sydney, New South Wales, came to England and became known as a racing cyclist. Promoted the Napier car and achieving some notable racing victories, including the only British victory in the Gordon Bennett Cup series (1902). In the 1920s, backed AC and Cubitt cars.

FLANDERS, Walter *(1871–1923)*
One of the US car industry's first mass-production experts. He was hired by Ford as production manager in 1908, but left in 1909 to found EMF. Later, he founded the United States Motor Company group.

FORD, Henry *(1863–1947)*
Son of an immigrant Irish farmer, Henry Ford wanted to lift the drudgery off farm life, and became an engineer in Detroit. In 1896 he built his first car. After two unsuccessful attempts to found manufacturing companies, he established the Ford Motor Company on June 16, 1903. He successfully defied the ALAM monopoly group.

FRANKLIN, Herbert *(1867–1956)*
Newspaper proprietor who became a pioneer of die casting, then in 1902 put the first air-cooled Franklin car on the market.

FRAZER, Joseph W. *(1894–1973)*
Having worked for Packard, GM and Pierce-Arrow, Frazer became President of Willys-Overland in 1939 and, with Henry Kaiser, founded Kaiser-Frazer in 1946 in an attempt to break the monopoly of the 'Big Three' in the popular car market.

HAYNES, Elwood G. *(1857–1925)*
Built his first car in 1894 with the help of the Apperson Brothers, and started the Haynes Automobile Company in 1898. He was also a pioneering metallurgist.

ISSIGONIS, Sir Alec *(born 1906)*
Designer of Morris Minor (1948), Mini-Minor (1959) and other fwd British Motor Corporation family cars.

JANO, Vittorio *(1891–1965)*
Italian designer for Fiat, Alfa Romeo and Lancia, for whom he created some of the finest sports and racing cars of all time.

JEFFERY, Thomas B. *(1845–1910)*
An Englishman who emigrated to the USA in 1863, and in 1879 began manufacturing 'Rambler' bicycles. He invented a 'clincher' tyre in 1891, and built his first successful car in 1900. Production of Rambler cars started in 1902.

JOHNSON, Claude *(1864–1926)*
First Secretary of the ACGBI (later the Royal Automobile Club). Introduced Rolls to Royce, and was first Managing Director of Rolls-Royce.

JORDAN, Edward *(1882–1958)*
A journalist who became Advertising Manager of the Thomas B. Jeffery Company, leaving to found the Jordan Motor Car Company in 1916. He became better known for his evocative advertising copy than for his cars.

KELSEY, Cadwallader *(1880–1970)*
Having built an experimental car in 1897, began production of Auto-Tri three-wheelers. Worked for Maxwell as Sales Manager 1905–09, then produced the Motorette car (1910–1912) and the Kelsey car (1921–1924).

KETTERING, Charles F. *(1876–1958)*
'Boss Ket' organized Delco laboratories to develop an electrical ignition system, and subsequently perfected the electric self-starter for the 1911 Cadillac. In 1920 he became head of the GM research laboratories.

KING, Charles Brady *(1868–1957)*
Built Detroit's first motor vehicle in 1896, and later designed the 'Silent Northern' and 'King 8' cars, turning to aeroengines in 1916.

LANCHESTER, Frederick *(1868–1946)*
British pioneer who built an advanced car in 1895. Apart from his contributions to automobile engineering, was one of the great pioneers of aeronautics.

LAWSON, Harry J. *(1852–1925)*
Company promotor, nicknamed 'Father of the British Motor Industry'. Attempted, from 1896, to form a patent monopoly to control the industry, and floated a number of overcapitalized companies, notably Daimler of Coventry (which survived the collapse of his empire in the early 1900s).

LEDWINKA, Hans *(1878–1967)*
Austrian designer who worked for Nesselsdorf, Steyr and Tatra, where he devised backbone chassis, all-independent suspension and air-cooled engines, latterly rear-mounted.

Hans Ledwinka

LELAND, Henry M. *(1843–1932)*
'The Master of Precision' learned his art in the arms industry. He also invented the mechanical hair-clipper and began building engines. He reorganized the Henry Ford Company as Cadillac after Ford resigned in 1902, later founding Lincoln.

LENOIR, J-J. Etienne *(1822–1900)*
A Belgian, he invented a successful method of enamelling clock faces in 1847, and in the late 1850s devised a gas engine. He built his first horseless carriage in Paris in 1862, later selling it to the Czar of Russia.

LEVASSOR, Emile *(1844–1897)*
Co-founder of Panhard-Levassor and inventor of the *Système Panhard*, in which the engine was at the front, under a bonnet, driving the rear wheels via a sliding-pinion gearbox. Died as a delayed effect of a racing accident.

MARKUS, Seigfried *(1831–1898)*
Austrian inventor who built a number of experimental internal combustion-engined test-benches from 1868. His first true car, long claimed to have been built in 1875, is now known to date from the late 1880s.

MAXWELL, Jonathan Dixon *(1864–1968)*
Starting in the cycle industry with Elmer Apperson, he worked on the 1894 Haynes-Apperson. In 1903, he joined Ben Briscoe to found the Maxwell-Briscoe company.

METZ, Charles *(1864–1937)*
Famed for his Orient cycles, Metz began production of the crude Orient Buckboard. In 1909 he introduced the low-priced friction-drive Metz 22, sold initially for home assembly.

MORRIS, William *(1877–1963)*
Starting as an Oxford cycle agent, Morris (who became Lord Nuffield) built his first Morris-Oxford light car in 1912, and came to dominate the British motor industry in the 1920s. He was renowned for his philanthropy.

NASH, Charles W. *(1864–1948)*
An itinerant farm worker, Charles Nash joined the Durant-Dort carriage company, then moved to Buick with Billy Durant, becoming President of that company in 1910 and of the whole GM group in 1912. He left to take over Jeffery and transform it into the Nash Motor Company.

OLDS, Ransom Eli *(1864–1950)*
Claimed to have built his first steam car in 1896, and his first petrol car in 1894. Success came with the 1901 Curved-Dash Oldsmobile. He later founded Reo, and also invented an early motor mower.

PENNINGTON, Edmund Joel *(1858–1911)*
American 'mechanical charlatan', who 'invented' an airship in 1885, and produced a number of eccentric motor vehicles which defied normal mechanical laws.

PEUGEOT, Armand *(1849–1915)*
Son of one of France's leading ironmongers, Peugeot translated his firm's expertise in making steel rods to replace whalebone in crinoline skirts into the manufacture of cycles. In 1889 the Peugeot company built a steam car designed by Serpollet, but then constructed tubular-framed Daimler-engined cars, France's first production cars.

POPE, Albert Augustus *(1843–1909)*
Colonel Pope founded a successful cycle manufacturing group in 1879, and moved into the motor industry via electric vehicles as early as 1896. Pope's motor group was dragged down by the decline of the cycle business.

PORSCHE, Ferdinand *(1875–1952)*
Austrian designer for Steyr, Austro-Daimler, Mercedes, Auto-Union, Cisitalia and Porsche, he created the original Volkswagen in the 1930s.

Ferdinand Porsche

PORTER, Finley Robertson *(1872–1964)*
Designed the classic Mercer Raceabout, as well as FRP and Porter cars, becoming Chief Engineer of Curtiss Aircraft in 1919.

RENAULT, Louis *(1877–1944)*
Son of a rich Parisian button maker, Louis Renault rebuilt his De Dion tricycle into a shaft-driven voiturette in 1898, and received so many orders that he began production of similar vehicles. By 1900, Renault was building 350 cars a year and was established as one of France's leading makes. Louis Renault died in prison during World War Two, having been accused of collaborating with the Germans during the Occupation of France.

RIKER, Andrew L. *(1868–1930)*
Built his first electric tricycle in 1884, but did not begin production until 1899. In 1902 joined Locomobile to design their first petrol cars.

ROESCH, Georges *(1891–1969)*
Brilliant Swiss engineer who became Chief Engineer of Clement Talbot of London at 25, designing high speed tourers of great refinement.

ROLLS, The Hon. Charles Stuart
(1877–1910)
Interested in machinery from an early age, Lord Llangottock's youngest son was a pioneer motorist and racing driver who entered the motor trade. Anxious to sell a car bearing his own name, he joined with the engineer Royce. Rolls died in a flying accident at Bournemouth, having been the first man to fly the English Channel both ways.

The Hon. C. S. Rolls (*left*) and Henry Royce

ROYCE, Henry *(1863–1933)*
Electrical engineer who built a twin-cylinder car in 1903, and went on to construct the 'best car in the world' as well as some remarkable aeroengines.

SELDEN, George Baldwin *(1846–1932)*
A patent attorney who experimented with engines from 1873 to 1875, and designed a self-propelled vehicle on which he filed a patent in 1879, the patent being granted in 1895. He sold the patent to Columbia Electric on a royalty basis in 1899, when it was used to try and create a monopoly group (Association of Licenced Automobile Manufacturers).

SERPOLLET, Léon *(1858–1907)*
Frenchman who devised the flash boiler for rapid production of steam, and built a steam tricycle in 1887. He built a number of steam three-wheelers in the 1890s, but did not seriously begin car production until the turn of the century. His sprint racers broke many speed records. His aim was to build a steamer that was as simple to control as a petrol vehicle, but his death from consumption ended the Serpollet company.

Frederick Simms

SIMMS, Frederick R. *(1863–1944)*
Brought the first Daimler engines into Britain in 1891, and fitted these power units into motor launches on the Thames. Formed the Daimler Motor Syndicate in 1893, which was taken over by Lawson interests in 1896. He invented the name 'motor-car', and helped to found the Automobile Club of Great Britain and Ireland (later the Royal Automobile Club) and the Society of Motor Manufacturers and Traders. He also built Simms cars.

SLOAN, Alfred P. *(1875–1966)*
At Durant's behest, formed the United Motors Corporation of accessory manufacturers, which was later absorbed by GM. An administrative genius, Sloan reorganized the corporate structure of GM, becoming its President from 1923–1936.

STANLEY, Francis E. *(1849–1918)* **and Freelan O.** *(1849–1940)*
The Stanley twins used the proceeds from the sale of their photographic dry-plate business to develop a steam car, the rights to which were bought for $250,000 to create Locomobile. The Stanleys came up with an improved design, Stanley steamers being built into the 1920s.

STUTZ, Harry *(1871–1930)*
Designed an improved rear axle, then became Sales Manager for Schebler carburettors, engineer for Marion and designer of the American Underslung. Manufacture of Stutz cars began in 1911; Harry Stutz resigned in 1919, later founding HCS. He was also a talented saxophonist.

THOMAS, Edwin Ross *(1850–1936)*
Though he founded the E. R. Thomas Motor Company in Buffalo, NY, in 1900 (it built the Thomas Flyer which won the round-the-world New York-Paris Race of 1908), Edwin Thomas never learned to drive.

VOISIN, Gabriel *(1880–1973)*
French aviation pioneer who went into car production between the wars with advanced and unorthodox sleeve-valve cars.

WHITE, Windsor *(1866–1958)*, **Rollin** *(1872–1968)* **and Walter** *(1876–1929)*
Rollin and Windsor built the first White Steamer in 1900, and Walter was sent to London the next year to develop the European market. Rollin left the White Company (Windsor was its President) in 1914 to build Cleveland tractors, and launched the Rollin car in 1923.

WILLS, Childe Harold *(1878–1940)*
A brilliant metallurgist who helped Henry Ford develop his first cars (and also designed the famous 'Ford' script logo) and became Chief Engineer of the Ford Motor Company. He developed vanadium and molybdenum steel alloys for the motor industry. With his severance pay from Ford he founded Wills Ste Claire. In 1933 he became Chrysler's chief metallurgist.

Childe Harold Wills

WILLYS, John North *(1873–1933)*
In 1906 undertook to sell the entire output of Overland, then mounted an effort to save the company when it got into difficulties in 1907, moving production to Toledo. He built Overland production up to 95,000 units – second only to Ford – in 1915.

WINTON, Alexander *(1860–1932)*
Scots marine engineer who jumped ship in America in 1880, starting bicycle production in 1896. Built his first car in 1896, founding the Winton Motor Carriage Company next year. In 1903, he launched an eight-cylinder 'Bullet' racer. His designs featured pneumatic controls. When car production was suspended in 1924, he began manufacture of diesel engines.